Toward A Primary Medical Care System Responsive to Children's Needs

HARVARD CHILD HEALTH PROJECT

VOLUME I

Harvard Child Health Task Force Members

Robert Bennett

Professor of Law
Northwestern University School of Law
Chicago, Illinois

John A. Butler

Assistant Dean for Academic Affairs
Harvard Graduate School of Education
Cambridge, Massachusetts

John Graef, M.D.

Associate in Medicine
Children's Hospital Medical Center
Boston, Massachusetts

Theodore Marmor

Associate Professor
School of Social Service Administration;
    and Research Associate
Center for Health Administration Studies
University of Chicago
Chicago, Illinois

David S. Mundel

Associate Professor of Public Policy
    (on leave)
John F. Kennedy School of Government
Harvard University

Barbara Starfield, M.D.

Professor and Associate Professor of
    Pediatrics
Department of Health Care Organization
Johns Hopkins University
Baltimore, Maryland

Richard F. Tompkins

Program Officer
The Cleveland Foundation
Cleveland, Ohio

Toward A Primary Medical Care System Responsive to Children's Needs

Report of the Harvard Child Health Project Task Force

Ballinger Publishing Company • Cambridge, Massachusetts
A Subsidiary of J.B. Lippincott Company

This book is printed on recycled paper.

International Standard Book Number: 0—88410—507—5

Library of Congress Catalog Card Number: 77—3387

Printed in the United States of America

Library of Congress Cataloging in Publication Data

Harvard Child Health Project.
  Toward a primary medical care system responsive to children's needs.

  (Its Harvard Child Health Project ; v. 1)
    1. Child health services—United States. 2. Medical policy—United States. I. Title. [DNLM: 1. Child health service—United States. 2. Child care. 3. Primary health care—In infancy and childhood. WA320 H339h]
  RJ102.H37a   vol. 1   362.7'8'0973s   [362.7'8'0973]
  ISBN 0—88410—507—5   77—3387

Contents

List of Figures

List of Tables

Foreword

Americans profess and believe that the well-being of children is given top priority in our family life and social policies. It is thus a cause of dismay and perplexity to most of us whenever facts suggest that the value we place upon children is not matched by a commensurate record of performance in their behalf.

But the evidence of disparities between our values and our actions concerning children is both solid and troubling. It is especially apparent in the arena of health and medical care. This decade has witnessed remarkable gains in access to physician services throughout the population, but when we analyze the data, we find that the nation's children have not shared adequately in this progress.

The gap between physician coverage among children from low-income families and doctors' visits by the rest of the population remains distressingly large. And because one child in every four—some 17 million in all—lives in poverty, this discrepancy poses a problem of substantial and sobering dimensions.

The stakes in narrowing the gap in the distribution of child health services are high. It is not merely a matter of relieving the immediate suffering of the millions of children who do not receive the care they should have. It is also a matter of improving the health status of the next generation of Americans. Childhood illnesses left undetected and untreated have a good chance of resulting in an adult life impaired by chronic and often disabling handicaps. Both the afflicted person and society are the losers. Human potential is left unfulfilled;

and the costs of expensive medical care and loss of work time and productivity are high.

The particular tragedy of these human and social costs is that, in a significant number of instances, they are preventable. The diseases of childhood, while they may be serious, are seldom the rare diseases. They are well known and many are amenable to decisive medical intervention.

Why, then, does the performance of our child health services fall so far short of the need?

Part of the answer rests in the essential difference between children's position with respect to getting care, and that of adults: namely, the fact that children are dependent on the decisions and help of others, especially mothers, in obtaining needed care. Today, adults responsible for providing the health stewardship children require are encountering increasing difficulty in discharging this function. The barriers include:

- The increasing scarcity of neighborhood-based primary care doctors, especially in the inner city and rural areas.
- The separation of families from helping relatives and grandparents.
- The large number of job related family moves.
- The increase in working women, which has brought half of all mothers into the labor force.
- The growth in single-parent households, now the home of one out of six children.

All but one of these barriers to placing children under care—the first—will require changes in our society that are largely beyond the helping capacities of medicine and health. Yet, that is no reason why our health professions and institutions should not move promptly on the issues that come within their domain. What this means specifically is the development of systems and arrangements for a coherent structure of general medical care addressed to the special requirements of children.

This is the theme of the Child Health Project launched in 1973 by a team of scholars organized by the Harvard University Graduate School of Education. The project team consisted of experts from clinical pediatrics, epidemiology, economics, early education, law, and other fields. With the help of an advisory committee, the group has completed a thorough-going study and analysis of the status of child health and health care in the U.S. It had also identified the critical public policy questions—manpower supply and distribution, financing and reimbursement patterns—in need of resolution if

American children are to have what their health most requires: the benefit of an organized system of accessible and appropriate primary care.

The findings of the authors of the Harvard Child Health Project are reported in this three-volume study. The Robert Wood Johnson Foundation is pleased to have provided the funding necessary to enable the Harvard group to accomplish what proved to be an arduous and exacting study and writing task.

It is our hope that this study will contribute to the ability of parents, physicians, nurses, civic leaders, and officials at all levels of government to ensure that every American child receives the best possible chance for a healthy start in life.

David E. Rogers
President
The Robert Wood Johnson Foundation

✻

Preface

The purpose of the Harvard Child Health Project was to review and analyze the findings of available research on children's primary medical care and to develop the policy implications of these findings. Our effort was divided into two stages. First, we reviewed the evidence in a number of areas of children's medical care treatment, delivery, utilization, and financing. These findings are summarized in the two background volumes that accompany this volume. Second, we met as a group to develop the policy implications of our findings. This volume reports these implications.

Our hope is that the three volumes resulting from the project can assist policymakers—private and public, nonphysicians and physicians—in designing a medical care system responsive to the needs of children. Whether or not these designs are implemented is inherently a matter of choice, not a result of research. Our research can help to make these choices more informed and thus more effective.

A number of individuals deserve much credit for our efforts. The staffs of the Robert Wood Johnson Foundation, particularly Robert Blendon, and of the Harvard Graduate School of Education and the Kennedy School of Government, particularly Deans Paul Ylvisaker and William Capron, provided substantive and emotional support throughout our efforts. The advisory group to the project, whose members are listed at the end of this preface, provided extensive and useful guidance throughout our research. The authors of the studies that provide the basic research for our findings provided key input for this summary. Our staff, particularly Judy Baumann, provided tireless assistance, unerring guidance, and a firm editorial and dead-line-enforcing hand. Our spouses and children should also be thanked for putting up with weekends and evenings of meetings and writing.

The views expressed in these volumes are solely those of the authors and do not represent, in any way, the position of either the Robert Wood Johnson Foundation or the institutions with which the authors are affiliated.

List of Advisory Committee

William M. Capron (Chairman)

Associate Dean
John F. Kennedy School of Government
Harvard University
Cambridge, Massachusetts

Robert J. Blendon

Vice President
The Robert Wood Johnson Foundation
Princeton, New Jersey

Marian Wright Edelman

Children's Defense Fund
Cambridge, Massachusetts

Peter Edelman

Director
New York State Division for Youth
Albany, New York

Leon Eisenberg, M.D.

Maude and Lillian Presley Professor; and
Chairman of the Executive Committee of
   the Department of Psychiatry
Harvard Medical School
and
Senior Associate in Psychiatry
Children's Hospital Medical Center
Boston, Massachusetts

Howard Hiatt, M.D.

Dean
Harvard School of Public Health
Cambridge, Massachusetts

Gilbert Steiner

The Brookings Institution
Washington, D.C.

Homer Wadsworth

The Cleveland Foundation
Greater Cleveland Associated Foundation
Cleveland, Ohio

Kerr White, M.D.

School of Hygiene and Public Health
Johns Hopkins University
Baltimore, Maryland

Paul N. Ylvisaker

Dean
Harvard Graduate School of Education
Cambridge, Massachusetts

Toward A Primary Medical Care System Responsive to Children's Needs

HARVARD CHILD HEALTH PROJECT

VOLUME I

Chapter 1

Summary and Conclusions

Children present different health problems and thus have special medical needs quite different from those of adults.

Current government policies are not well directed toward fulfilling these special needs. Current policies concentrate on financing (thru Medicaid and Medicare); pay less attention to purposeful changes in the delivery system; and direct research and development attention to "heroic" medicine. If medical care is to be more responsive to children's needs, their special problems must be fully considered in designing changes in both the medical care system and the public and private policies that influence it.

Children are sick more often than adults, but their illnesses are generally less serious and are often self-limiting. However, some children are very sick, and some children's illnesses, although minor, may become very serious and destructive. For example, strep throat can result in rheumatic fever if left unattended, and recurrent middle ear infection (otitis media) can result in significant hearing loss. Children's medical needs also differ from those of adults because their problems more often relate to development, for instance, sexual maturation and learning processes. Such development-related conditions are sometimes classified as part of a "new morbidity" because traditionally they have not been a focus of attention within the medical care process.

Children's illness patterns indicate a need for a primary care focus in the medical care system. Children need continuing and comprehensive medical attention aimed at prevention—care that prevents frequent onslaughts of childhood diseases and care that prevents childhood diseases from becoming more severe or disabling. The concentration of adult-oriented medicine and medical policy on hospitalization and high technology sources of care is not an appropriate response to the needs of children.

Unequal patterns of morbidity and medical care usage among groups of children are also problems confronting the health care system. Minority children and children from lower-income families are ill more frequently than their white and upper-income counterparts. Minority, central city, and lower-income children use care less frequently than white, suburban, and upper-income children. This inequality contrasts with the equalization of medical care usage rates among adults which has occurred in the last decade. Disadvantaged children use medical care less frequently, are less likely to use preventive or primary care, and are more likely to wait for symptoms to become severe before seeking medical assistance. Any proposed change in the medical system must be carefully considered in light of the special needs of these groups of children with more illness and lower service utilization rates.

Some evidence apparently casts doubt on the effectiveness of primary care for children. Several studies have shown that more physicians and more physician visits do not necessarily reduce illness and death rates. Taken together these studies provide support for the increasingly accepted hypothesis that medical care has "no effect" on health status. Some observers believe that the "no effects" findings with respect to children result from the "fact" that most childhood illnesses are "self-curing or self-correcting" and thus not influenced by medical care. Another hypothesis that can explain these "no effects" findings is that although medical treatment is efficacious for childhood conditions (it can prevent, ameliorate, and cure), it is not delivered in an effective manner. Although the "no effects" and "self-correcting" hypotheses appear to raise the most concern for the medical care system because they question its basic premises, the "ineffective delivery" hypothesis is even more disturbing. Basically, this hypothesis implies that the current system is not delivering efficacious care—even to the children with whom it comes in contact; even when potentially productive treatments are available.

Primary care involves much more than simple medical treatment of illness and the provision of immunizations. First, the existence of a problem must be *recognized*. Recognition of the existance of problems most often comes from talking with patients and their families. It also is derived from knowledge about children and their surroundings, by astute observations and examinations and from screening procedures. Opportunities for problem recognition occur during visits of children for illness or well-child care, and physicians' experiences in the community in which children live, work, and play. After a problem's existence is recognized, it must be *diagnosed* in order to locate its cause and develop a policy for cure and amelioration. The curing and amelioration process involves *treatment, management,* and *compliance.* In order to assess whether or not the medical process has resulted in cure, *follow-up* procedures must be undertaken. Each of these components of the primary care cycle must be performed well if the cycle of care is to be effective.

In many instances and for many conditions, components of the primary care cycle are not adequately performed. Problem recognition is one of the most poorly and most underperformed functions. Middle ear infections and lead poisoning are common, particularly among disadvantaged children, and their consequences can be severe. Yet these problems often go unrecognized even among children who see medical care providers. Extensive screening programs are often implemented, but the accuracy and validity of screening tests are highly uncertain and poorly understood. The back end of the cycle of care—follow-up—is also generally inadequately provided, if provided at all. Most primary care clinics and private office-based care providers rarely follow up on patients, and thus the accuracy of problem recognition and diagnosis, the positive effects of treatment, and the thoroughness of compliance are not assessed. Too often a problem in one of these areas remains undetected. The current primary care system is less than fully effective, not because medical care has no or little effect on childhood illnesses, but because all the components of the full cycle of care are not adequately provided, even to those children who receive care.

The low utilization of primary care by poor and minority children, in comparison with others and with professionally assessed needs, results from imbalances between demand and supply. Utilization of primary care depends on several factors, particularly price, distance and time, and whether or not a child has a regular source of care. Each of these factors affects the use of primary care services by disadvantaged children.

The price of care matters more for children from poor families than for others; the price of primary and preventive care is a more effective deterrent of utilization than is the price of other health services; and fewer poor children are covered by private and public programs that pay for nonhospital, primary care services. Distance and time are more important inhibitors of the use of primary care than of the use of other services, and poor children live farther from their care providers and have to wait longer for appointments than other children. If children have a regular source of care, they are more likely to use primary/preventive care services adequately, but lower-income children are less likely to have care-providers that they use repeatedly and regularly. For all these reasons, lower-income children use primary care services less frequently than middle-income and upper-income children.

The supply of primary care—in the aggregate, for particular groups of children, and in particular neighborhoods—is also an important determinant of utilization. The chief factor of supply is the number and distribution of primary care practitioners, largely physicians. The number of physicians who provide primary care to children has been declining (in terms of MDs per 100,000 children). The types of physicians providing primary care to children has been changing from general practitioners (GPs) who frequently practice alone in offices, to pediatricians who, like other specialists, prefer group practice arrangements with hospital and other institutional affiliations. The percent of physician time devoted to primary care is also declining. These trends have reduced the availability of primary care for children in general, and for poor, central city, and rural children in particular, because they are at the end of the market queue for service.

Three policy directions are indicated by the diverse reasons for low utilization of primary care services: first, increases in the quantity of primary care services delivered; second, changes in the location and types of units delivering primary care; and third, changes in the financing of primary care services. There are several ways of achieving each of these desired changes. The quantity of primary care services delivered can be increased by expanding the pool of primary care physicians, by increasing the productivity of the practice arrangements of primary care physicians, and by increasing the numbers of nonphysician practitioners who deliver primary care services. The second and third of these alternatives are highly connected and are likely to be more effective and less costly than the first. Nonphysician primary care practitioners (e.g., pediatric nurse practitioners) can substantially increase MD productivity and deliver high quality care that is accepted by patients. Several factors inhibit the use of these practitioners: few of them have been trained; reimbursement from public programs cannot always be made for the services they perform; several states restrict nonphysicians from practicing without direct, on-site supervision by MDs; and most primary care physicians have not been trained to productively use these types of personnel in their practices. Each of these barriers must be lowered if nonphysician practitioners are to be used effectively to expand the responsiveness of the primary care system to children's needs.

Changes in the location and modes of primary care delivery are more difficult to achieve. Federal categorical health programs have achieved some success in developing health care units (e.g., neighborhood health centers) in previously underserved communities. Some of these, when properly staffed and managed, have resulted in improved primary health services and health status. Efforts to encourage practitioners to locate in underserved communities through service contingent training subsidies, legal requirements, or direct financial subsidies have not been generally successful. Without much larger subsidies, stronger requirements or restrictions, their potential for success is low. Improvements in the ability to pay for care among residents in underserved areas, such as that induced by Medicaid in lower-income communities, do not appear to offer substantial incentives for increased supplies of primary care services. If more primary care services are to be brought to children in underserved areas, direct federal support for new delivery units (providing the full cycle of care and utilizing nonphysician practitioners extensively) will be required. At a minimum, support during the initial development of these units, and continuing until they become self-financing through capitation or reimbursement, must be provided.

Direct government financing of patient care services is the third method through which the medical care system's responsiveness to children's primary care needs can be improved. The current public and private financing programs emphasize hospital services either through limitations of coverage or deductibility requirements which are high enough to omit most primary care services financed by out-of-pocket payments. These eligibility and coverage limitations are also present in several national health insurance proposals currently under consideration. If primary care services are to be increased, they must at least be eligible and covered for reimbursement, especially for lower-income children.

Current financing systems emphasize fee-for-service modes of reimbursement and these may be counterproductive, or at least not very productive, for encouraging children's primary care services. Fee-for-service reimbursement emphasizes explicit patient services, but many components of the cycle of primary care—especially problem recognition and follow-up—are not easily subjected to either cost analysis or billing. If the full cycle of care is desired then this is the "service" for which reimbursement should occur. A system of capitation payments (one payment for service to a patient over a period of time) is one possible mode of financing the complete cycle of children's primary care that should receive more attention.

The performance of these possible policy changes—emphasizing the full cycle of primary care and increasing the utilization of non-physician primary care practitioners; increasing support for new delivery modes in underserved areas; and improving the financing of primary care services—is by no means certain. Therefore, if the medical care system's responsiveness to the special needs of children is to be improved, research and development in the area of children's primary care must be undertaken. Currently, most medical research concentrates on treatments for severe illnesses, and most of these affect adults. Improved capacities to recognize, diagnose, and treat childhood illnesses are necessary if the primary care system is to be effective. Research on and experimentation with delivery and financing alternatives should also be directed toward children's primary care in order to improve our understanding of the effects of policy alternatives on this sector of care. Children's health is a special resource and it should be given more than general or passing attention in the medical care research, development, experimentation, and policy design and implementation processes.

Chapter 2

The Special Needs
of Children

This report sets forth the implications of making children full partners in the nation's health care enterprise. National health care policy has not always had as positive an effect on children as on other groups in the population. Children have special medical needs, quite different from those of adults, yet these needs were not taken into full account when the government expanded its role through the enactment of Medicaid and Medicare a decade ago. Nor was attention paid to the changes occurring in the types of illnesses experienced by children or to the differential effect of policy alternatives on the utilization rates of children versus their effect on adult utilization behaviors. As a result, little effort was made to relate children's medical needs to the financing and organization of health care.

In the future, it is vitally important that any programs of national health financing, delivery, and regulation fully reflect the interests of children. This is not to argue that children's needs should be given priority over the needs of other groups, but rather that the special nature of their needs be considered in making changes in health delivery and financing systems.

Attention must be directed to the kinds of problems that may become serious later in life if left untreated in childhood; to warding off chronic and disabling illness, or at least ameliorating their effects; and, through preventive care practices, helping children to move successfully through healthy childhood into healthy adulthood.

Data on children's illnesses illustrate the differences in the health needs of children as opposed to adults. Children get sick more often, but their illnesses are generally less serious and are often self-limiting. Morbidity and mortality statistics for children also show a disturbing gap between the health status of nonwhite and white children and between that of poor and well-to-do children. For example, the incidence of infectious diseases for nonwhite children has not lessened to the extent it has for white children. In one sense, the pattern of illness for nonwhite children is similar to the pattern exhibited by white children a decade or more ago. The improvement for white children is evidence of improvements in the health status of children, but it is clear that this advance has not reached all segments of the population.

There are also growing numbers of children with chronic or handicapping conditions whose conditions need effective management. Further, there are a number of problems that stem from manmade environmental problems; socioeconomic problems, such as drug-abuse; and the problems connected with sexual maturation in our modern society. Finally, the area of learning disabilities is becoming a medical issue, even if only because parents are seeking advice of doctors when their children fail to perform up to their expectations.

The implications of children's health care needs are obvious. *To be effective for children, the nation's health care system must pay increasing attention to primary health care.* Unfortunately, as we shall see the health care system that has evolved has not emphasized primary care needs because of current policies toward medical care financing, types of delivery units, and medical personnel. *Further, the health care system must find ways to bring those children who are now outside the system, or at least benefiting less from it, into the health care system.* Financing mechanisms, delivery units, and personnel policies must be designed with this target population—the poor, nonwhite, and central city children—clearly in mind.

THE CYCLE OF PRIMARY MEDICAL CARE

The cycle of primary care is entered when there is a perceived need to deal with a situation, a "problem." This recognition leads to the marshaling of various types of evidence, from the history, physical examination, and laboratory procedures, which point to a diagnosis. The diagnosis is the name given to an abnormality in the function and/or structure of body organs or systems. This diagnosis facilitates the planning and application of a strategy of treatment and management of the problem. The process does not end here, for there must be a subsequent reassessment. Was the therapy effective? Was the problem resolved? Is there a new problem, to initiate a new cycle?

This cycle of care is the same for children as adults, although at some points young children's inability to articulate their symptoms may compound the difficulties.

There is a serious lack of evidence about the impact of the cycle of primary health care on children who receive this care. There has been almost no attempt to understand the relationship of the various components of the cycle of care to each other, and to pinpoint weaknesses in the cycle of care. The Harvard Child Health Project examined several common conditions of childhood in an attempt to determine what is known about the cycle of care and where the problems persist. From this research, it is evident that the areas of problem recognition and follow-up are *particularly* weak links in the cycle of children's care. Further, the emphasis of the biomedical research field on "exotic" diseases rather than on the more common complaints of childhood represents a weakness in our current efforts to improve the effects of the medical care cycle for children.

UTILIZATION OF HEALTH CARE BY CHILDREN

The other question besides the general one of whether the cycle of care is effective is whether the clients of the system have access and entry into the system according to their individual health status and needs. Do the clients take advantage of preventive care services? Do they respond early to symptoms and seek proper care for their condition or wait until treatment becomes more difficult, costly, and perhaps less effective? Do they comply with prescribed treatments and cooperate in follow-up procedures? The effectiveness of the system depends not only on the diagnostic and treatment procedures but also on the interaction of the clients with the system.

From the statistics on morbidity and mortality it is clear that services may not be equally accessible to all segments of the society. Utilization data confirm the unequal use of medical care services by nonwhite children, as well as by the poor and those living in central cities. Further, the data show that while there has been a trend over the last decade toward equalization of use rates for the population as a whole, for children the gaps in utilization have not narrowed to the same extent. This seeming failure of the system in regard to children is tied in some measure to the financing and delivery mechanisms now in effect.

Examining the utilization patterns of American children, one finds that utilization of primary medical services by nonpoor and white children is substantially higher than that of poor and nonwhite children. From studies done on whether children do see a doctor when they, in fact, "need" to, it appears that low-income children do not receive care as often as their symptoms would appear to warrant. Lack of a regular source of care is one reason for these inequalities. Seven percent of American children have no regular source of care. Children from low-income families are almost eight times as likely to have no regular source; nonwhites more than three times as likely as whites; and those living in the central cities one and one-half times as likely as those in the suburbs.

Several factors affect utilization of health care both by adults and by children. One is the price. Over the past decade there have been a number of attempts at the federal level to equalize access to care by financial subsidies such as Medicaid and other categorical assistance programs. These programs have had an effect. But for children there are other factors which also exert a considerable influence over whether or not a child will receive care. Perception of the need for care is one such factor, and for children, it is the parents' perception of need that is required. Distance from a health care site and time spent waiting for a doctor once at the site are two factors that appear to have more of an impact on children's health care utilization and the type of care sought than on that of adults.

The problem of reducing the inequalities and maldistributions that characterize the primary health care system can be approached as an issue of demand and supply. On the side of *demand*, the failure to seek care by some segments of the population is a problem. What are the constraints on demand? The most obvious is the price of care. Reducing prices is the approach taken in the creation of the Medicaid program. But the "costs" of health care surpass the dollar amount requested in return for the services given. The distance travelled, time spent waiting, and the anxiety surrounding a health care visit are also important "cost" factors affecting the demand for care.

On the *supply* side, several forces are at work in the delivery of primary health care to children. There must be adequate health care providers, both in numbers available and their proximity to their clients. Numerous programs of the federal government, such as the National Health Service Corps, the Comprehensive Health Manpower Act of 1971, Medical Services Act of 1975, and Health Professions Educational Assistance Act of 1976, have been designed to improve the supply of physicians.

Putting the right mix of delivery services nearer to potential consumers of primary health care is another option to improve the supply structure. This is the approach taken in the federal government's efforts to create neighborhood health centers and in other public programs.

PERSONNEL ISSUES CONFRONTING DELIVERY OF CHILDREN'S HEALTH CARE

The presence of powerful magnets elsewhere in the U.S. system have served to draw personnel and other resources away from primary care, to distort the distribution of primary care providers, and to cause inefficiencies that affect the adequacy and appropriateness of these services and raise their costs.

One of the magnets is the attraction exerted on the medical profession to specialize rather than to go into more general, primary care practice. This has led to the decline of the general practitioner, traditionally the bulwark of primary care in the United States. Medical students have been attracted strongly to the various surgical and clinical subspecialties by the prospects they see for increased financial rewards, greater prestige, and more interesting and absorbing careers. While there has been a marked increase recently in the numbers of practicing physicians who serve the primary care area—pediatricians, internists, and the newly created category of family specialists—this increase has not offset the losses in primary care providers caused by the declining pool of general practitioners.

Many physicians have been attracted to research and other functions rather than to practice. Pediatricians have been attracted to hospital practice in nonprimary care areas. For many specialists the teaching hospitals, particularly those in large medical complexes associated with universities, offer opportunities for training, residency, research facilities, and backup by the vast resources available to major hospitals. This has influenced not only the supply of physicians available at other sites, but also the total number available to serve patients directly.

Because physicians have been attracted to where the affluent markets and amenities of life are to be found—the suburbs—there is a shortage of office-based primary care physicians in central cities as well as in rural areas.

Many of the functions of primary care physicians could be handled, at least in part, by nonphysician health personnel. The development of such personnel—pediatric nurse practitioners, child health associates, and others—would increase the productivity of primary care physicians and, as a result, increase their effective number. This is particularly important for children because of their need for primary care services.

The decline of the general practitioner has meant a decline in office-based care. More people are using hospital outpatient clinics and emergency rooms as their sources of care. These sites are usually equipped for secondary and tertiary care. Further, because of the need for technologically sophisticated, hence expensive, equipment, there is a need to consolidate the resources of these centers. This places them farther away from their clients.

FINANCING HEALTH CARE FOR CHILDREN

Children receive less of a share in the direct public subsidies for health care than their numbers would appear to warrant. As the nation's system of delivering and financing health care services is now constituted, children suffer a double deficit. First, the financing system is designed mainly for the needs of adults. This applies both to public programs such as Medicaid and to private health care insurance plans as well. Second, the financing of health care has perversely affected the problem of the availability and distribution of primary care services.

Total national expenditures on personal health care in 1975 were an estimated $103.2 billion, of which $15.4 billion was accounted for by children under nineteen years of age. Although the under-nineteen group comprises some 30 percent of the nation's total population, they account for only 15 percent of expenditures on physicians, and 8 percent of expenditures on hospitals. In part, this discrepancy can be explained by the differences in the general health status and needs of children as compared to those of adults. But this explanation is only partial. There are biases within the health care system, particularly in its financing, that work against the interests of children as a group.

Thirty-three percent of children's expenditures went for hospital care and 33 percent for physicians' fees. This is in sharp contrast to the general pattern of health care expenditures. For all age groups, 45 percent of total expenditures went to hospitals and only 21 percent to physicians. The differences in the expenditure patterns of the under-nineteen group and those of adults reflects in general the differences in needs of the two groups, including the large component of primary care received by children in nonhospital settings.

One reason for the discrepancies between subsidies for adults and for children is the bias in the financing system favoring institutional care, which children need less than adults. But beyond this, it reflects still a further bias in the kinds of practitioner services that are subsidized. Only some aspects of treatment are covered. Many routine preventive care needs, particularly those supplied by nonphysician health practitioners, are not covered by the reimbursement schemes designed primarily with hospital costs in mind.

There is little doubt that the changes in the delivery and financing of health care over the past several decades, particularly in the establishment of the Medicaid program, have improved medical care for many disadvantaged and minority children. But because the conditions forced on the system have not been fully compatible with the needs of children, they have not yet experienced the same degree of improvement that has occurred in the delivery of care to other groups.

SPECIAL LIMITATIONS OF CHILDREN

Children as a group have special limitations that affect their entry into the health care system. They are limited in their ability to make decisions for themselves with regard to health care, and children as a group have no leverage on the decisions affecting health care policy. They can't vote; they are not organized into groups acting as a force to make their needs known. Children are represented generally through their parents, who in the past have had wide control over the individual decisions affecting the kinds of treatments to be administered to their children.

As the government has taken on more of a role in the financing and delivery of health care of children, there has been a trend away from absolute parental consent requirements as a prerequisite to medical treatments. For example, the Supreme Court has recently held that absolute parental consent cannot be required for a minor's abortion.

Children are still very dependent on their parents knowing their best interests. In general, parents must recognize where a problem exists, present the problem to an appropriate health care provider, and follow up by administering the treatment in conformity with the doctor's instructions. Children, through their parents, are beginning to take more of an active interest in how the health care system functions, for example, through advocacy efforts to monitor existing delivery systems and federal programs. Because the health care system is perceived to be a complex system where the doctor alone "knows" the right thing to do, however, children are for the most part dependent on the medical care provider to manage appropriately their medical care problems, and on systems dominated by adults to find ways to finance, deliver, and regulate their health care.[a]

A cautionary note, however, serves as a reminder that children's needs cannot be considered separate from the needs of the population as a whole. We know that our present system of care is fragmented, and any system designed with children's best interests in mind must not further fragment the delivery of health care or children will suffer in the end. By and large, however, the problem is that children's needs are not fully considered by those who are in a position to improve the cycle of care for children, and the utilization and delivery of that care.

To achieve an effective system of delivering primary care to children, the major medical care policies—stimulating demand, opening up access to delivery, enlarging the medical care labor force, as well as improving productivity—must reflect the special needs of children.

[a]The legal implications of trends in decisionmaking in children's health care are discussed more fully in Robert Bennett's chapter in volume III of this series; the role of advocacy groups in promoting children's interests in health care is discussed in Richard Tompkin's chapter in the same volume.

Chapter 3

Changing Patterns of Death and Illness Among Children

Statistics on illness in children, while better developed in the United States than in other countries, have not been systematically collected over a sufficient period of time, nor are they classified in such a way as to yield useful analysis and interpretation. Comparative statistics on mortality, on the other hand, have been collected for many years. Therefore, the most reliable statistical approach to the state of health of U.S. children, ironic though this may seem, is through statistics on death.

CHANGING CAUSES OF DEATH

There have been radical changes since the 1930s in the causes of death in children under fifteen. The end of the 1930s marked a transition in the history of child mortality in the United States. The greatest decline in death rates in this century occurred before 1940 and can be attributed largely to environmental improvements and better living standards (Newberger et al., 1976). From 1937 on, following the introduction of antibiotics and chemotherapy, the over-all childhood mortality rate continued to decline, but at a slower rate. But there have been dramatic changes in the relative incidence of life-threatening illnesses. Figures 3–1 and 3–2 show the shifts in the five leading causes of death in childhood at intervals from 1939–41 to 1974. These figures indicate the extent to which social and environmental factors are major causes of injury and death in children. Indeed, accidents and homicides cause nearly twice as many deaths in

Figure 3–1.   Five Leading Causes of Death in Children from the Ages of One through Four, 1939–41 to 1974 (rates per 100,000 population).

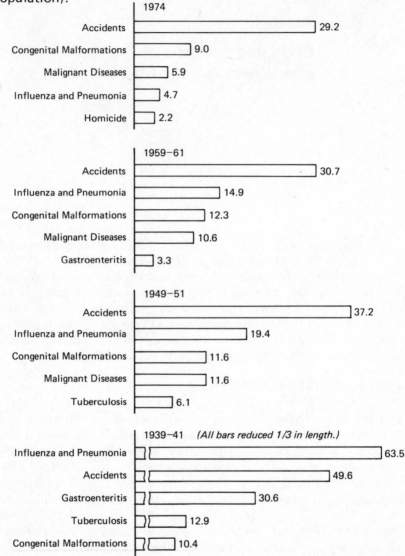

Source for 1974: National Center for Health Statistics. Advance Report, Final Mortality Statistics 1974 (HRA) 76–1120, vol. 24, no. 11, Supplement, 3 February, 1976.

Source for other years: Shapiro, S.; Schlesinger, E.; and Nesbitt, R., Jr. *Infant, Perinatal Maternal and Childhood Mortality in the United States.* (Cambridge, Ma.: Harvard University Press, 1968), p. 175.

Note: Alaska and Hawaii included for 1959–61 and 1974.

Figure 3–2. Five Leading Causes of Death in Children from the Ages of Five through Fourteen, 1939–41 to 1974 (rates per 100,000 population).

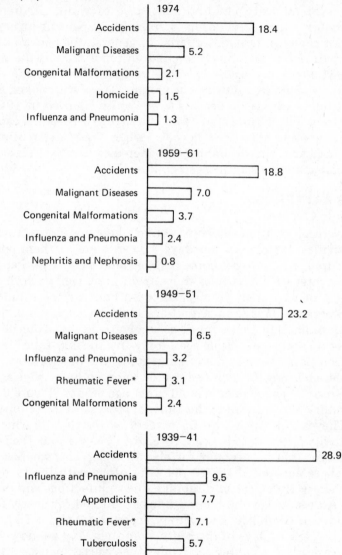

*Includes rheumatic heart disease.

Note: Alaska and Hawaii included for 1959–61 and 1974.

Source for 1974: National Center for Health Statistics. Advance Report, Final Mortality Statistics 1974 (HRA) 76–1120, vol. 24, no. 11, Supplement, 3 February, 1976.

Source for other years: Shapiro, S.; Schlesinger, E., and Nesbitt, R., Jr. *Infant, Perinatal, Maternal and Childhood Mortality in the United States.* (Cambridge, Ma.: Harvard University Press, 1968), p. 177.

the five-through-fourteen groups as all the other eleven leading causes of death combined.

Equally significant and disturbing are the disparities between death rates of minority children and those of white children. The death rate for minority children is roughly 50 percent higher than the rate for their white counterparts. In general, the pattern of leading causes of death for nonwhite children tends toward the pattern of white children a decade or more earlier. Rheumatic fever and rheumatic heart diseases illustrate the point. These still ranked among the five leading causes of death for nonwhite children in 1959–61 although they had disappeared from the listing for leading causes of death among white children a decade earlier. This pattern of mortality rates indicates the desirability of increases in the availability of primary care among disadvantaged children.

ILLNESS PATTERNS

On the average, children under fifteen are kept by illness from their usual activities for almost ten days a year, four of them spent in bed.[a] Children from lower-income families tend to have poorer health and higher rates of illness than those from more well-to-do families.

As might be expected, younger children have a greater number of restricted activity days than school-age children. Children under five suffer approximately three times as many bouts of acute illness in the course of a year as people aged forty-five to sixty-four.[b] School-age children have twice as many ailments as the older group. Taken as a whole, children through the age of fourteen have twice as many acute illnesses a year as people in all other age groups (Figure 3–3).

Respiratory ailments are by far the major cause of acute illness disability. They account for over 55 percent of the days in which children's activity is restricted owing to acute illness, about the same as ten years ago. Injuries account for about 13 percent, whereas a decade ago these accounted for 10 percent. Along with the increase in injuries there is a decline in disability due to infectious and parasitic diseases. A decade ago these conditions accounted for nearly 22 percent of days of disability; today they account for about 16 percent. About 3 percent of days of disability were then, and are now, due to digestive conditions. Disabilities from other causes increased from 9 to 12 percent.

[a]The major source of comprehensive information on acute illness in children is the National Health Survey, which is conducted by the National Center for Health Statistics.

[b]The material for this chapter and the next is found in volume II of this series.

Figure 3–3. Incidence of Acute Illness by Diagnosis and Age.

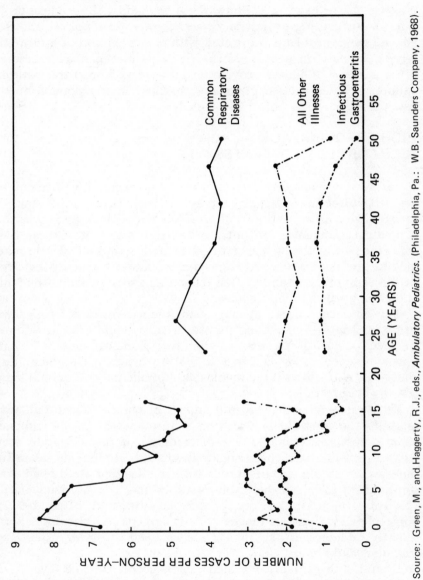

Source: Green, M., and Haggerty, R.J., eds., *Ambulatory Pediatrics*. (Philadelphia, Pa.: W.B. Saunders Company, 1968).

These data are inadequate in many respects: they do not indicate the severity of the illnesses; the categories are too broad; and there is no clue regarding the relationship of the disability to the organic or physical factor causing it. Illnesses not treated by the medical profession or not causing restriction of activity are not reported, and there are the usual problems associated with the collection of information relying in part on people's memory of past events. Yet these and other surveys of illness provide valuable insight into the nature of children's illnesses as compared with those in the population as a whole.

HIGH FREQUENCY OF SELF-CORRECTING ILLNESS

It has been estimated that many episodes of acute illness in children are self-correcting (Haggerty et al., 1975). That is, the child will recover without any serious aftereffects regardless of whether there is medical intervention or not. In this large majority of cases, therefore, the role of the physician or other medical attendant is primarily helping the family or child cope with the illness, reducing the effects of the temporary disability, and reassuring and supporting the family and child until the illness abates.

The emphasis placed by physicians themselves in the past several years on the self-correcting nature of most childhood acute illness has been a useful reminder to the profession that much of what it seems to accomplish is owed to nature instead. This reminder at times has also led both the medical and public policy communities in the wrong direction.

We do not yet know the full impact of childhood morbidity and disability on subsequent health or performance of young adults, because we have virtually no understanding of the extent to which adult problems have their origins in childhood ailments. Even such illnesses as middle ear infection (otitis media) that are thought to be self-limiting may not be. Abnormalities may persist (sequelae, in medical terminology) in an appreciable proportion of children as a consequence of various illnesses. This happens so often and is so frequently undetected that there is a clear need to devote attention to its causes and effects.

Even if the estimates of high incidence of "self-correcting" ailments prove accurate, they do not necessarily indicate a limited role for medical care. First, the capacity to predict which cases will respond favorably to treatment and which will self-correct is almost totally lacking. Second, the long-term consequences of childhood illness and of the self-curing process may be significant. Thus, high likelihood of self-correction may not be enough to allow the withholding of treatment from sick children. Furthermore, medical care provides both curing and caring—the lessening of discomfort and anxiety—and the value of this second set of effects should not be underestimated.

At one time, management of the episodes of acute illness was the central concern of the system; now the focus must be on the ability of the system to provide a long-term (or longitudinal) perspective on child health care. More stress must be placed on procedures for reassessing children after their acute illness episode to make certain that there is no unhappy aftermath; effort must be redoubled in assuring that common illnesses, which are relatively easy to treat in their acute stage, do not progress to chronic conditions.

CHRONIC ILLNESSES AND THE "NEW MORBIDITY"

The large and growing numbers of children with chronic or permanent disabilities show that serious ailments are somehow escaping detection by the medical profession or are failing to be adequately managed. This resistant hard core of serious ailments in children represents a growing challenge to medicine. When the system fails to ward off preventable disabilities, the later costs in terms not only of human discomfort and suffering but of economic loss as well are burdensome to individuals and society.

According to the estimates of Nathan B. Talbot and Andrew Guthrie, one out of every ten American children suffers a handicap severe enough to require some sort of remedial service. About 1.7 million children and youths under twenty-one in 1970 had crippling health impairments, including congenital cardiovascular disabilities, cerebral palsy, epilepsy, diabetes, and asthma. An estimated 2.8 million were mentally retarded; another 1.5 million were suffering from psychological disturbances. Some 2.2 million had speech impairments, 200,000 were blind or partially sighted, 500,000 were deaf or hard of hearing, and 750,000 had learning disabilities (Talbot and Guthrie, 1976).

Many of these problems are increasing for complex reasons going beyond the inability of the medical system to deal adequately with acute illness. Talbot and Guthrie point to the broader definitions of handicapping and to more widespread application of diagnostic procedures. They also note the far higher survival rate of children who, in earlier years, would have died soon after birth. Some of the increase reflects the growing hazards and stresses children face in American society today.

This raises the complicated and elusive problem of how to deal with the varied afflictions that have been bundled together under the heading of the "new morbidity," which covers a range of illnesses and disabilities arising from social, behavioral, and environmental problems. Robert J. Haggerty includes in his definition roughly four groups of physical and emotional difficulties that cause parents to seek medical help for their children or sometimes impel children to seek it for themselves. These groupings overlap and are not easily defined.

The first set of such problems is related to schooling and may be behavioral in part but often involves learning disabilities. Another general problem concerns sexual maturation in adolescence, heightened by tensions growing out of a drive for independence from the family. A third set of problems arises from manmade environmental hazards, such as air pollution, lead poisoning, and unsafe toys. And finally there are the emotional and physical problems caused essentially by economic conditions and current social instabilities, often involving drug and alcohol abuse (Haggerty et al., 1975).

Some of the problems lie largely, though not exclusively, outside the realm of traditional medical practice, for instance, reading disability. It is estimated that as many as 15 or 20 percent of school-age children have reading problems. Dyslexia, minimal cerebral dysfunction, and developmental dyslexia are examples of some thirty terms that have emerged from the research over the years in an attempt to classify children who have reading problems. But the development of this terminology tends to be misleading; it gives the impression that there are specific syndromes of reading disability and implies that the syndromes can be attributed to some physiologic abnormality. At this stage of medical research and treatments, reading disability is one of many childhood problems that are susceptible neither to precise definition, certain recognition or diagnosis, nor highly effective treatment (Longfellow and Freeman, 1977).

Although many problems included in the "new morbidity" may be primarily in the province of nonmedical personnel—for instance, educators—it is clear that physicians have been and will become increasingly involved with them. Increasing numbers of worried parents and children come to family physicians and pediatricians about these problems. Many of them have pathophysiologic correlates and have repercussions on the child's health, both organic and functional. The great challenge confronting the medical profession and those doing research into these problems is to develop techniques leading to more precise and sure recognition of the problems and more accurate diagnosis of disabilities by primary care practitioners. Even if these disabilities are not treated at this level of care, these practitioners must be prepared to refer patients to the appropriate type of therapy at other levels and in other modes of care, and to follow-up on the results of the care received elsewhere to assure that it is adequate and effective.

Chapter 4

Flaws in the Cycle
of Primary Care

In theory, increases in health services should lead to an improvement in the health status of children. Proper prenatal care should reduce the incidence of congenital defects and infant mortality. Many acute childhood diseases might be entirely prevented by appropriate management of the conditions that precede them; for instance, the treatment of strep throat with an appropriate antibiotic may prevent rheumatic fever. A number of studies have attempted to determine what difference, if any, is made in health status by differences in the amounts and kinds of medical care children receive. The results of these studies have not been reassuring.

Several studies have investigated the effect of increased physician-to-population ratios and higher physician-visit rates on mortality and morbidity rates. The results of these studies are generally inconclusive. For example, Senior and Smith (1972) and others have found little relationship between infant mortality rates and physician-to-population ratios.

Other studies have investigated the effects of different types of care on morbidity characteristics. Alpert and his colleagues at the Harvard Family Health Care Program followed the children of six hundred families over a period of three years. Half of this group received health care in their usual fashion (through the Boston Children's Hospital emergency room and clinics) and half, the experimental group, received care from a team consisting of a physician, nurse, and social worker at the Family Health Care Center. After three years the groups showed no difference in morbidity nor in total numbers of physician visits (Alpert et al., 1968).

More recently David Kessner and his associates in Washington, D.C. studied six-to-eleven-year-olds who had different sources of care. They found that three common primary care conditions— middle ear infection (otitis media), vision defects, and iron-deficiency anemia—were present among children of comparable socioeconomic status regardless of the type of medical care provider utilized and were high for all socioeconomic groups. "Differences among the patients, rather than differences in how those who delivered care were organized," concluded the researchers, "had the predominant influence on health status of children (Kessner et al., 1974, p. 3).

This general finding—little observable connection between either medical care availability or utilization and health status—has two possible explanations. Either childhood illnesses are not amenable to cure by medical care or there are widespread defects in the cycle of primary care. Current evidence indicates that for some conditions there are identifiable defects in the cycle of care. For example, there is no question that antibiotics can be highly efficacious when appropriately administered. But there is a question as to whether they are being effectively administered for maximum usefulness and minimal unintended effects.

Kessner's findings highlight the importance of isolating and identifying as precisely as possible where and why the failures and successes in medical practice occur. They raise basic questions about the effectiveness of the various functions within the primary care cycle, from problem recognition and diagnosis through treatment, case management, compliance, and finally follow-up. The findings also raise questions about the relationship of the participants to the medical care system.

Why do health conditions fail to respond to medical intervention? One possibility is that the understanding of the problem—recognition—by the practitioner fails to reflect the nature of the problem as it exists in the patient. Another possibility is that techniques of diagnosis or treatment applied are not in themselves efficacious—a failure of the art of treatment. It may be that the health care provider failed to apply the procedures properly. Or perhaps the patient failed to comply with the prescribed treatment. Still another possibility is that existing techniques are not capable of revealing whether intervention has or has not brought about some effect.

One way to cut through the problem is to make a distinction, as is increasingly done in research in the field, between "efficacy" and "effectiveness," efficacy having to do with the outcome of specific diagnostic and therapeutic procedures, effectiveness with the degree to which the system achieves generally accepted goals.[a] Medical procedures are efficacious when they are shown by scientific evidence to be useful under optimum conditions. Whether these procedures are applied adequately or produce the intended results is a question of effectiveness. Effective medical care can be said to occur only when there is adequate problem recognition, diagnosis, management, and follow-up of treatment; this implies the full participation of all involved, those who receive as well as those who provide treatment.

The Harvard Child Health Project employed the efficacy-effectiveness distinction in making a detailed study of several childhood health conditions. The purpose was to see what could be discovered about the efficacy of the steps now taken by the primary care system in treating typical illnesses and whether these do or could lead to effective medical intervention. Five of these studies, summarized here, were concerned with middle ear infection; lead poisoning (plumbism); strep throat (streptococcal pharyngitis and its sequelae); iron-deficiency anemia; and tonsillectomy and adenoidectomy. Each of these studies illuminates different aspects of the difficulties involved in problem recognition, diagnosis, treatment strategy and reassessment, and in the relationship of these functions to other functions in the system. Collectively, they yield valuable insights into flaws in the current cycle of care and the appropriate design of a responsive primary medical care system for children.

MIDDLE EAR INFECTION: PROBLEMS OF RECOGNITION AND FOLLOW-UP

Middle ear infection is one of the most common ailments of childhood, particularly in children under ten years of age. It is the third leading reason for visits to pediatricians, after well-child care and immunization. Some 75 percent of all middle ear infections are self-limiting, and antibiotics have made such severe complications as mastoiditis rare. Notwithstanding, middle ear infections account for an estimated 50 percent of all hearing loss in childhood. Its role as a major factor in learning problems and poor educational progress has been recognized since the time of pioneering studies in Britain in the 1930s.

Recognition of middle ear infection has been a major problem. Diagnosis through use of the otoscope, for many years the accepted practice, is unreliable. However, a new technique that measures ear

---

[a]For a fuller discussion of *efficacy* and *effectiveness*, see "Efficacy and Effectiveness of Children's Primary Medical Care" by Barbara Starfield, M.D., in volume II of this series.

drum pressure (tympanometry) has been introduced and gives promise of greatly improving the accuracy of diagnosis. Treatment of middle ear infection is accomplished either through surgical drainage or antibiotics. There is a controversy over the liberal use of antibiotics because of the inherent danger of undesirable side effects and also in view of the high degree of self-correcting infection. In general, however, treatment, if indicated, can be regarded as efficacious once this condition has been recognized.

Even allowing for these inadequacies in procedures, the main problem appears to be a failure of the medical system to practice at the present state of the art. Reliability in recognizing evidence of the disease is low. Many cases of infection are missed, even though doctors are alert to the illness because of its prevalence. Studies also indicate that the record of physicians in assuring a good response to management is spotty. According to one study, only 40 percent of children with recognized cases of infection received a follow-up examination within two weeks following diagnosis, and only 7 percent were seen within the optimum period of from ten to fourteen days. Compliance with prescribed treatment by patients is generally poor. Physicians rarely follow up with hearing tests to screen for impairments to hearing even when a history of infection should lead them to suspect a problem.

This evidence indicates that the delivery system can be indicted for its poor record in handling middle ear infection. It is essential to concentrate greater resources and effort on the improvement of problem recognition, which lies at the root of much of the ineffectiveness in primary care for children.

Improving problem recognition by health practitioners will accomplish several things. It will enable them to sort out more effectively the large proportion of illnesses that are self-correcting and permit these cases to be handled more appropriately and efficiently. As has often been pointed out, neither highly sophisticated professional expertise nor elaborate equipment is required to cope with self-correcting ailments. The task is to lend support and comfort to the children and parents and to assure as comfortable, speedy, and complete a recovery as possible. This has consequences for the kinds of technical skills and levels of competence that are required in dealing with the acute illnesses in children.

Even more important, improved problem recognition will identify more certainly the far smaller number of cases of serious acute illness or chronic conditions on which the medical profession should be expending its fullest capability and energy. At the same time, the system will be able to handle more effectively and efficiently the greater load of patients that will occur when those not now being served adequately or at all are brought into the system.

LEAD POISONING: INADEQUATE LEVELS OF RECOGNITION

Lead poisoning is unusual, if not unique: it is a manmade, environmental disease; its causes are well known; and it can be readily identified as long as people are alert to it. It is caused by old lead paint in dilapidated housing and to a much lesser degree by lead-contaminated dust along heavily traveled highways. Treatment is definite and efficacious, but if the child is to be saved from irreversible and serious damage, recognition of the problem must occur early. When the symptoms appear, it may be too late. Lead poisoning is therefore a case where the medical system cannot merely let victims walk in the door: it must go out and seek diseased children if they are to be spared the consequences.

Lead is highly toxic and affects the bone marrow, kidneys, and nervous system; untreated, lead poisoning can be fatal. It symptoms are similar to those of other diseases with which it can be confused. If not caught early, before symptoms appear, it can produce serious physical and behavioral problems, including seizures, cerebral palsy, and mental retardation. There are an estimated 400,000 cases of lead poisoning in the United States, almost all among children under six years old in urban areas. There are 150 to 200 deaths a year from the disease.

Society has two possible choices in regard to lead poisoning. The first is to remove the lead in the environment by rehabilitating the old housing that is the major cause of the problem, but this is a costly choice which would require billions of dollars. There is little possibility of such a course of public action being taken on a massive scale, although there are some federal and state programs for rehabilitating such housing. The second choice is to provide continuous screening of children who are in the so-called target group, children who live in areas where there are large numbers of deteriorated houses and who are likely to ingest flaking and peeling lead-based paint.

The nation has in fact chosen the second option. Such a screening program on a national basis was begun in 1972 under the Childhood Lead Poisoning Control Program. Its target group comprises 2.9 million children between one and six years old. Screening has proven effective in detecting cases of lead poisoning and in leading to a reduction of the disease through treatment programs. However, in the first two years of the program, less than 25 percent of the target group had been screened. Since both early detection and continuous testing are essential to the effectiveness of such screening, the present program clearly falls short of what should be expected of it. The problem here is that even when an effective system for early recognition is available, it is less than universally implemented.

One issue raised by the problem of lead poisoning is the extent to which the health care system itself should become involved in case finding. This issue is also present in other new morbidity problems. Should the health care delivery system restrict itself to testing the blood of at-risk children? Or should it become involved in initiating inspection of possible lead poisoning sources? As our society deals more and more with this and other new morbidity problems, research is needed into the most efficient ways to locate and recognize such problems.

SCREENING

Screening is a method of problem recognition. Its purpose is to separate from a large group of apparently healthy children those who are at increased risk of having a given condition. It is intended to provide early recognition of conditions that can impair a child's later development. Its use on a mass scale has been advocated on the grounds that it provides an entry into the medical care system for those not having a regular source of care and that early treatment may be less burdensome for the patient in the long run and less costly for society.

Screening thus offers the possibility of applying mass techniques to the key medical function of problem recognition. However, there are a number of serious problems and unanswered questions about mass screening that should be considered in formulating policies. Because the tests for many illnesses are imprecise, there can be and often are errors in recognition. If the errors lead to identification of a problem where none exists, there are unhappy human consequences in terms of the needless anxiety caused when children and parents are led to believe that a condition is present. This type of error also overloads medical treatment providers. If the error is in failure to identify a problem that exists, it leads to missed opportunities for cure and a false sense of security.

At this stage in the development of screening techniques, the best likelihood of success would appear to occur when two conditions are present: first, when the objective is to locate a specific condition known to exist in an identifiable group of high-risk children; second, when the test itself is known to be sensitive and specific. Screening for hearing loss as a result of middle ear infection and lead poisoning fall in this category. The wide application of screening to uncover a variety of other incipient ailments and disabilities should be approached very cautiously. Screening is a medical tool of great potential that must still be studied and researched intensively before its potential can be fruitfully realized.

STREP THROAT: A PROBLEM IN DIAGNOSIS AND TREATMENT

Strep throat presents first a problem of diagnosis. Infections of the throat are one of the most common of all childhood ailments, but only a very small number of these infections, perhaps 5 percent, are streptococcal. These infections, however, can result in scarlet fever or, far worse, rheumatic fever. The greatest incidence of rheumatic fever occurs between the ages of six and fifteen, with a peak at eight years. The fever and other symptoms of streptococcal throat infections are much the same as in other throat infections, with the consequence that examinations by physicians are subject to a high degree of misdiagnosis. The problem lies in securing a positive identification of the disease in order to determine whether to apply the treatment or not. Fortunately, there are highly efficacious treatments for strep throat, in particular the use of penicillin. But if penicillin is prescribed out of hand, it will be redundant in perhaps three-quarters of cases.

The customary diagnostic procedure, therefore, is to take a throat culture and test it. But this does not always produce accurate results, and further complications are encountered in interpreting the results. A positive culture will not reveal whether the child will develop an immunity to the streptococcus. Nor, on the other hand, will it reveal whether the child will become a carrier for a prolonged period. Final judgments about strep throat, therefore, are often made on the basis of the results of the culture along with other factors. These include taking into account white blood count, previous history of infection, the infections of siblings, and so forth.

Recently, Richard Tompkins and his associates conducted a study based on three different diagnostic and treatment approaches: give throat cultures to all patients and treat positive cultures with penicillin; treat all patients with penicillin; or do nothing (Tompkins et al., 1976). They concluded that under ordinary circumstances treating all patients who have acute pharyngitis is more efficient than treating only those who have positive cultures. The incidence of rheumatic fever is less, and the procedure is more economical. Serious penicillin allergy would occur in a relatively small number of cases, but there would probably be no deaths. The number of cases of serious allergy would probably exceed by only a very small fraction the number that would occur under the procedure of treating those with a positive culture—three to nine additional cases in 100,000 patients.

This type of care could clearly have far-reaching effects on effectiveness of treatment, allocation of resources, and efficiency. But the broad-scale use of antibiotics runs against the grain of much opinion in the medical profession. Nevertheless, approaches such as this appear to warrant extensive study because of the possibilities they hold for increasing the over-all effectiveness of the cycle of primary care.

What this clearly indicates, as in the case of middle ear infection, is the need for far greater emphasis on clinical research in the common diseases of childhood. Most of the attention in clinical research now is focused on more esoteric conditions to the neglect of the familiar ailments of childhood. The tendency for research to concentrate heavily on "exotic" conditions and diseases is not unique to this particular area of research of course; it pervades the whole of medical research. Clinical studies in streptococcal infection and other familiar ailments—particularly upper respiratory diseases—are urgently needed if effective primary health care is to be delivered to children.

IRON-DEFICIENCY ANEMIA: FAILURE OF RECOGNITION, MANAGEMENT, AND FOLLOW-UP

Anemia is the most common blood disease among infants and children in the United States. Large-scale surveys indicate that 14 percent of all children are anemic and that iron deficiency is the cause of this condition in the great majority of cases. As the most widespread nutiritional deficiency in the United States, it has its highest incidence among lower-income groups in both rural and urban areas. Iron-deficiency anemia presents no particular problem in diagnosis; hemoglobin tests yield excellent results. Nor is there doubt about the efficacy of supplementation therapy, the only real question being how best to administer the dosage, orally or by injection.

There are, however, problems in the recognition (screening), management (treatment), compliance, and follow-up stages of the cycle of care for iron-deficiency anemia. One study, for example, showed that whereas 70 percent of doctors associated with medical care organizations routinely screen for the disease, only about a quarter of solo physicians do; and only a quarter of children using outpatient departments of hospitals were screened.

Problems of compliance and follow-up, although significant in many of the areas of primary care, are subordinate in the case of iron-deficiency anemia to another more basic issue: Does treatment, efficacious as it may be, get at the underlying implications of the problem? The question concerns the relationship of iron deficiency to functional impairment and to behavioral problems, in particular to learning problems. There is great difficulty in separating the effects of iron deficiency from other conditions that are often present and may be related to the various symptoms observed, ranging from fatigue to gastroenteritis. The difficulty is all the greater because of the prevalence of the condition among poor children, who are likely to be suffering from one or more of these related conditions. Research has often been unable to determine whether decreased body-iron levels are a cause or effect of the conditions with which they are found to be associated. This failure to cope adequately with iron-deficiency anemia in a wide variety of research studies conducted over a period of time indicates a need for intensive clinical research on this common childhood ailment.

TONSILLECTOMY AND ADENOIDECTOMY: UNWARRANTED TREATMENT

Tonsillectomy and adenoidectomy (T and A) surgery offers a dramatic illustration of what can happen when a lag in clinical knowledge combines with a failure within the delivery system itself. T and A is the most frequently performed operation in the United States and the most frequent cause of hospitalization in children. There are some one million T and A operations annually in this country, with a human toll of complications for many children and even of death in some instances. The economic cost of using these tertiary care solutions for substantially primary care problems is estimated at some $350 to $500 million annually, a major diversion of medical resources to this one surgical area. There is little if anything in the entire literature of medicine to justify such a risk or cost.

Questions have been raised about the efficacy of T and A since the 1880s, and yet the operation is still performed for a variety of reasons ranging from the presence of upper respiratory and middle ear infections to general underdevelopment of the child associated with repeated tonsil infection. The many studies that have been made are contradictory regarding the value of T and A; some studies have even indicated that there are benefits in *not* having the tonsils and adenoids removed. Yet the significant fact is that in all these years no thorough study has been undertaken to determine definitively the function of the tonsils (and adenoids) and more efficacious approaches to supporting its presumed role in acting as a first line of defense against respiratory infection.

There are startling variations in T and A surgery rates from one country to another, and even from one locality to another within the United States. These differences cannot be explained by the incidence in occurrence of any conditions that might require surgery. The more likely correlation, as in surgery generally, is between the numbers of hospital beds and surgeons available in proportion to the population. Collaborative efforts within the medical profession through such means as peer review can bring the rates for T and A down sharply. Vermont offers an example. In 1969, the variation between T and A rates in different localities of Vermont ranged as high as ten to one. Since then, the medical profession in Vermont has set up new criteria for tonsillectomy and has initiated joint review of all cases by both pediatrician and surgeon prior to a decision to operate. In three years, there was a drop of 46 percent in the statewide surgery rate for T and A, and the range of rates among areas narrowed significantly.

Beyond the clinical implications involved in tonsillectomy and adenoidectomy, there is a further important lesson for the medical profession: There must be a flow of information from one level of the medical system to another. In this case, there must be close collaboration between primary care physician and surgeon. The system, to be both effective and efficient, requires monitoring at some point where the child's complete health needs are understood and recorded and where responsibility on the patient's behalf will be exerted.

IMPLICATIONS FOR THE CYCLE OF CARE

The findings about the state of children's health care in this chapter strongly indicate that the present cycle of care is not responding adequately to children's needs as these must now be defined. Three areas in particular show significant failures to achieve adequate response.

First, as is abundantly clear, problem recognition is becoming a matter of increasing concern. A problem is a stimulus that should initiate a chain of events on the part of the health profession. Timely and complete recognition of this stimulus is a prerequisite to the stock and trade of the medical profession: the diagnostic and therapeutic process. If problems are not recognized properly the diagnostic and therapeutic process, no matter how internally logical, will be inappropriate or erroneous. Unfortunately, we find that problem recognition is often deficient. Greater capability must be developed in the medical profession for early recognition of problems that signal the onset of chronic ailments or disabilities and impairments in childhood and subsequently in adulthood.

Second, there must be greater follow-up in the treatment of acute illnesses, to prevent later complications from arising; and clearly, greater attention must now be paid to the long-term chronic diseases and permanent disabilities.

Third, greater capacities must be developed to respond appropriately to the health problems that children have, including those of the new morbidity, and to provide care, not simply cure, for the high numbers of ill children and their families.

Chapter 5

Inequalities in the Utilization of Physicians' Services

American children under seventeen average four visits to physicians each year, but the levels of utilization differ greatly for different groups of children. Some of these differences in utilization are easily explicable in terms of the child's health status; others are not. The patterns of children's visits to physicians in 1972 are shown in Table 5–1.

The far greater number of children under six visiting physicians compared with the number of school-age children is accounted for by the far higher rates of morbidity among these children and their higher utilization of well-child visits. In the aggregate, children under six make twice the number of visits that older children do, which is in inverse proportion to their total numbers in the population. But no such reasoning can explain the disturbing differences between the amount of primary medical care received by children from low-income families compared with that received by children from higher-income families. These disparities, clearly indicating higher use by higher-income groups, exist for both younger and older children.

There are also marked disparities in the use of physician services according to where the child lives: in city, suburb, farm, or rural non-farm areas. Children living in suburbs, as might be expected, receive more services from office-based physicians than those in central cities or rural areas. The disparities are more marked in the case of older children. Visits to dentists reflect the same general disparities for rich-poor and city-suburb-country that are seen in the utilization of physician services.

The utilization of primary medical services by white children is

Table 5–1.   Health Care Utilization by Children According to Family Income and Place of Residence, 1972

	Percent under Six Years with One or More Visits to:			Percent Six to Sixteen Years with One or More Visits to:		
	Physician	Dentist	Hospital	Physician	Dentist	Hospital
Family Income[a]						
Under $5000	79.9	9.5	9.7	52.8	37.9	4.3
$5000–9999	85.9	13.8	7.1	60.0	52.5	4.7
$10,000–14,999	89.2	22.3	7.8	66.9	66.9	4.9
$14,000 or more	91.3	29.9	7.7	72.3	79.2	4.0
Total	86.3	17.5	8.0	63.7	60.8	4.5
Place of Residence						
SMSA[b]						
Central city	87.6	16.1	8.0	63.8	56.6	4.4
Outside Central City	88.8	21.0	7.9	67.2	67.3	4.2
Rural Nonfarm	83.2	14.8	8.1	61.0	56.9	4.9
Farm	79.2	19.1	7.4	52.4	57.2	4.0
Total	86.3	17.5	8.0	63.7	60.8	4.5

[a]Includes children with family income unknown.

[b]Standard Metropolitan Statistical Area.

Source: "Current Estimates from the Health Interview Survey, United States, 1974," DHEW Publication Number (HRA) 76–1527, September 1975. Adapted by David S. Mundel, "Policy for Primary Medical Care for Children: a Framework of Basic Choices" (paper delivered at the 1975 Sun Valley Health Forum, Sun Valley, Idaho, August, 1975).

substantially higher than that of nonwhite children. In brief, children who are nonwhite, live in central cities, and come from low-income families receive less primary care than their more advantaged counterparts. But it is these very disadvantaged children who need *more* health care to compensate for their higher levels of illness and disability. Thus, comparisons of utilization rates understate the actual degree of inequality that exists with regard to unfulfilled medical care needs of different groups of children.

FOR POOR CHILDREN, A PERSISTENT GAP

These inequalities in utilization rates for children persist despite the broad trend toward equalization of medical service utilization that has occurred over the past several decades. This over-all trend results from several major developments in the private and public financing and provision of health care. The extension of private health care insurance coverage through Blue Cross and other private carriers to millions of American families has been one such factor in equalizing care. Largely employment based, this system of insurance has mainly affected employed middle and upper-income people and their families. The introduction of Medicare and Medicaid by the federal government in the mid-1960s provided financial assistance for medical care to older people and to large numbers—though by no means all—of lower-income people in the population.

The expansion since the 1960s of federal categorical programs that supply health care has to a lesser extent influenced the over-all trend toward equal utilization rates. These programs include the neighborhood health centers, Maternal and Infant Care projects, and Children and Youth projects. Together with Medicaid, these programs have greatly improved the access of poor children to medical services, though Medicaid has been by far the most important factor in bringing about the improvement in the utilization of services by children.

There is no question that utilization of physicians' services by different groups of children has become more equal since the mid-1960s. But whereas the annual rate of physician visits by lower-income adults now exceeds that of higher-income adults, lower-income children continue to have lower physician visit rates than higher-income children (Figures 5–1, 5–2, and 5–3).

For adults between the ages of twenty-five and sixty-four, there was not merely an equalizing of the numbers of visits by lower-income people as compared to those by higher-income people, but the patterns have actually reversed. In 1964, on the eve of the introduction of the federal medical assistance programs, adults in this age

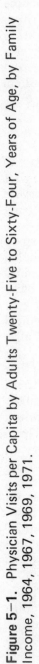

Figure 5-1. Physician Visits per Capita by Adults Twenty-Five to Sixty-Four, Years of Age, by Family Income, 1964, 1967, 1969, 1971.

An accurate comparison graph (all years adjusted to equivalent 1971 dollar value).

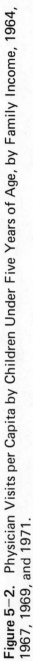

Figure 5-2. Physician Visits per Capita by Children Under Five Years of Age, by Family Income, 1964, 1967, 1969, and 1971.

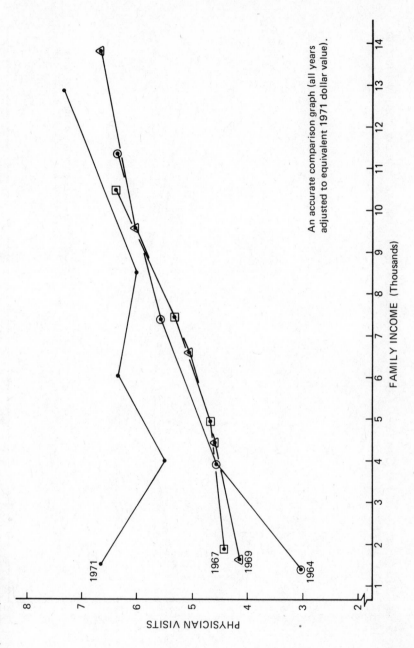

Figure 5—3. Physician Visits per Capita by Children Five to Fourteen Years of Age, by Family Income, 1964, 1967, 1969, 1971.

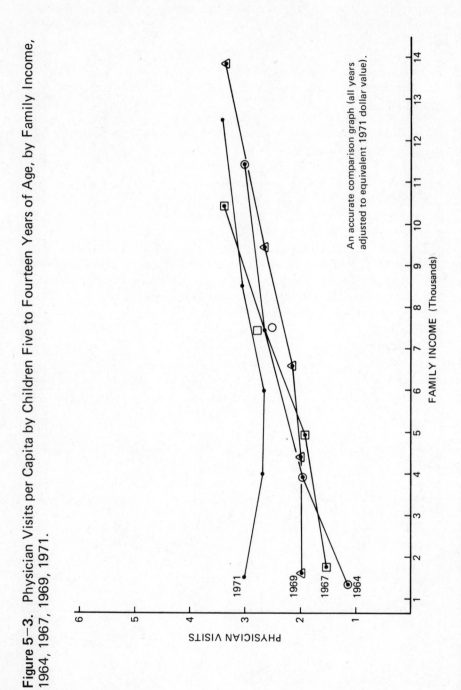

group at the low end of the income scale averaged slightly fewer visits to the doctor per year than the adults at the high-income end of the scale. By 1971, this had reversed.

But the utilization patterns still curve the other way for children. There is little question that for lower-income children utilization of physicians' services has improved since the mid-1960s. In 1971, children under five years old at the low end of the income scale saw physicians between five and seven times a year, a big improvement from 1964, when they averaged between three and five visits. Similar gains have been made by children from five to fourteen years of age. Nevertheless, in neither case have utilization rates for poor children become equal to those for children from better-off families—and much less have they exceeded them, as is the case for adults.

Despite their gains, children from poor families—the ones in the greatest need of remedial attention—are still less likely to receive as much medical attention as their more fortunate counterparts from higher-income families. Karen Davis recently summed up the situation in a different way. In analyzing the changes in the utilization of medical services by the poor since the introduction of Medicaid, she noted that progress has been

particularly evident for poor children, a third of whom had not seen a physician for two years or more in 1964. By 1973, this figure was reduced to one-fifth of all poor children. Despite this gain, however, poor children were still fifty-seven percent more likely not to have seen a physician in two years prior to 1973 than nonpoor children (Davis, 1976, p. 127).

The more serious the children's illnesses, the more the utilization patterns of poor families resemble those of nonpoor families. But visits for preventive, well-child, routine, and remedial purposes, or because of minor ailments, are often deferred by poor parents. It is meaningless, therefore, to talk of physician access solely in terms of numbers of available medical resources. Medical care services are in fact available to most persons at a cost, including not only the price of the medical care itself but also time, transportation, and psychological costs. And for the poor, these are frequently more onerous than for the nonpoor. These barriers have larger effects on the utilization of preventive and primary care services.

What basic factors influence the use of medical services by children?[a] This is the key question in seeking ways to improve the pri-

---

[a]Background for this section can be found in the chapter by Diane Beauchesne and David Mundel in volume III.

mary care system for children. Apart from the degree of perceived need for medical care, parental attitudes regarding health and medical treatment are obviously important. Three other influential factors are the price of the service in relation to the family's income; distance from the child's home to the provider or health facility and how long it takes to get there; and waiting time to get to see the practitioner.

THE PARENTAL ROLE IN CHILDREN'S CARE

Under most circumstances, children's use of health services is determined by their parents rather than by the children themselves. Parents' knowledge of medicine and their attitudes toward it influence the entire process of primary care for children, from the recognition of illness and the selection of a provider, through supervising compliance with prescribed treatment and making sure that follow-up procedures are carried out. In the present fragmented system of primary health care, they also bear an important responsibility for functioning as the center of the network that passes essential information on their children's conditions from one part of the system to another. In brief, parents play a critical role not only in nurturing the good health of their offspring but also in determining the effectiveness of the medical care system and its ultimate outcomes.

In most instances, it is the mother who makes the initial decisions about seeking and carrying out medical care for the child. It has been shown that the attitudes of mothers toward health care and their behavior in regard to their own health are useful in explaining the differences in the utilization of health care among children. L.A. Aday reports that when mothers have not had a physical examination in the past year and are generally skeptical of the value of care, children are also less likely to have received a physical exam in the previous year (Aday, 1971). Studies by W.F. Dodge and colleagues likewise have shown that actual performance of mothers, in terms of seeing that their children receive tuberculosis skin tests and measles vaccine, accord with their views about health care (Dodge et al., 1970). Still another study indicates a high correlation between the feelings of alienation, powerlessness, and social isolation experienced by mothers and the immunizations received by their children. The greater the feeling of helplessness, the fewer the immunizations (Morris et al., 1966a).

Kessner's studies have shown that the differences in children's health status that can be attributed to educational and income differences among parents may often not be as great as is commonly believed (Kessner et al., 1974). He has reported that among children six months to five years of age whose mothers had less than a high school education, a third were anemic. Among children in the same age group whose mother had an education beyond high school, the proportion with anemia was lower, but still high: 20 percent. A similar result was observed in rates of hearing loss among children four to twelve years of age. Of those children whose mothers had less than high school education, 8 percent had hearing loss in frequencies that fall within the normal range of speech; the rate was 5.5 percent among the children whose mothers had received more than a high school education. Kessner goes on:

> It is equally disturbing and shocking to find that over 20 percent of children from families where total income was less than $5,000 per year had middle ear infections, while almost the same proportion (over 18 percent) of those with incomes of more than $15,000 per year had this disability. Similarly, for vision disorders there were no differences by social status. Thus, a very substantial amount of disease was found in even the upper-income families (Kessner et al., 1974, p. 2).

This emphasizes the widespread need for adequate education of parents of all income groups about the need of children for health care. The continued existence of the problems observed by Kessner results from a failure of recognition by the medical care system. Parents must be sensitized to needs for care and encouraged to see that these needs are fulfilled. This is an essential element in the interaction between clients and providers in the primary health care cycle.

THE EFFECT OF PRICE ON UTILIZATION

The broad effect of the various mechanisms for financing health care has been to insulate consumers from the full impact of prices. Mainly because of government subsidy programs, this is also generally true for the poor. But because of the way these subsidies are dispensed, it is less true for children than other age groups.

Despite increased financing of children's health care by private insurance plans and government subsidies (Medicaid), and the increased availability of free public health services, the price of health care still remains a barrier to the utilization of medical services by children. This barrier both reduces and distorts their levels of service utilization.

The average out-of-pocket payments for children's health care by the poor who do pay some expense is not very high relative to the costs of health care for others in the population (Table 5—2). But these costs are high relative to what the poor can afford. Hence, price still can affect the utilization of care by children from poor families.

These price effects can exist even for families eligible for Medicaid because of cost-sharing requirements under some Medicaid programs. Various states have established copayment arrangements for recipients of medical care that are intended to discourage overutilization of medical services by recipients of subsidized care. The fees involved are small—but not to families with low incomes or those already burdened with medical expenses which consume a disproportionately large share of their limited incomes.

Several studies have shown that even small out-of-pocket charges can significantly affect the utilization of primary care—ambulatory and preventive services—by lower-income families and children. A recent experiment with copayments for Medicaid recipients in California found that charges of one dollar for the first two visits to a physician reduced utilization rates. Ambulatory care use went down for those under copayment, and hospital use, while initially lower for copayment than for non-copayment beneficiaries, ended up being higher for the copayment group. The initial obstacle to ambulatory care retarded people's inclination to seek care until later in the cycle of illness, when required hospitalization became more expensive than it would have been with prompt treatment.

Welfare recipients showed the greatest reduction in physician visits as a result of required copayment. This means that poor mothers, and more importantly, children were not seeking care to the same extent as those who did not have to pay part of the cost of care. The case of immunizations is more disturbing. To the extent that copayment restrains young families from seeking preventive or other medical help, the program is affecting the wrong people.

Health care insurance plans as they are now constituted work not only against the interests of poor children, but against the interests of children as a class. Out-of-pocket payments and consumer cost-sharing requirements have an adverse effect on the use of primary care services by children. These payment arrangements even exist for families with private health insurance plans. Information collected by the National Center for Health Statistics shows that about three-quarters of all children were covered by hospital insurance under private plans in 1972, but slightly less than a third were covered for physician visits. The lower the income, the greater the discrepancy.

Table 5–2. Average Out-of-Pocket Costs of Health Care for Children under Seventeen Years of Age, by Family Income, 1970

| Family Income | Total Population (thousands) | Percent Distribution | | | | | | | Average Expense for Persons with Expense | Per Capita Expense |
| | | No Expense (parent) | Health Expense | | | | | | | |
			Less than $50	$50– 99	$100– 249	$250– 499	$500– 999	$1000 or More		
All incomes[a]	66,716	18.0	25.9	23.3	24.2	6.2	1.7	0.8	$128	$105
Less than $3000	5,387	47.4	28.7	11.9	8.1	*[b]	*[b]	*[b]	86	45
$3000–4999	6,677	34.4	30.2	16.2	15.1	3.5	*[b]	*[b]	89	58
$5000–6999	10,501	27.2	29.6	18.7	14.7	6.1	2.3	*[b]	153	111
$7000–9999	15,104	14.7	26.9	27.7	24.3	4.9	*[b]	*[b]	109	93
$10,000–14,999	18,497	6.8	25.7	26.4	31.4	6.8	1.8	*[b]	134	125
$15,000 and over	8,572	4.5	14.9	27.1	37.8	11.6	3.3	*[b]	161	154

[a]Includes persons with unknown incomes.

[b]Figure does not meet standards of reliability or precision.

Out-of-pocket costs include insurance premiums.

Source: *Monthly Vital Statistics Report*, vol. 22, no. 1, Supplement, 2 April 1973. Health Interview Survey—Provisional Data from the National Center for Health Statistics.

In families with incomes of $10,000 or more, 90 percent of children are covered by hospital insurance as compared to 41 percent covered for physician visits. For children in the $5000 to $10,000 group, the proportions were 71 percent and 24 percent. And in the under $5000 group, they were 30 percent and 7 percent. This lack of insurance coverage clearly discourages the use of those primary care services most required by children.[a]

HOW DISTANCE AND TIME AFFECT USE RATES AND PATTERNS

As we have noted, the use of medical services in cases of serious illness in children is not affected by the price of the services, nor by the other factors that influence utilization. Parents manage to get medical attention for their children when the need seems urgent. What all three factors—price, distance, and time—do affect, however, is the kind of service sought and where it is sought.

The distance that people have to go in seeking medical attention appears to distort rather than to reduce their use. After a thorough review of all the available data, L.A. Aday concluded that distance does not affect whether care is sought, but it does affect *where* it is sought. However, most studies on the impact of distance on health care utilization have examined only utilization by adults or have not sorted out the data by age groups (Aday, 1972).

Studies that have looked specifically at children's utilization have found that distance has a greater impact on the use of health services by children than by adults. According to a study by J. Weiss and colleagues, distance influenced the choice of site among a health maintenance organization's clinics more for pediatric visits than for visits by enrollees over eighteen years of age (Weiss and Greenlick, 1970). Transportation difficulties are often cited as the reason that wellchild appointments are missed (Morris et al., 1966b).

Certain differences in response to distance can be attributed to behavioral patterns relevant to social status. A Portland, Oregon, study of members of a health-maintenance organization found that subscribers who lived farther away from the site of care pay fewer scheduled visits to the clinic (Weiss and Greenlick, 1970). This was true for both middle-class and working-class clients. Where the middle-class clients compensated by making more phone calls to the medical personnel, the working-class clients tended to increase the number of unscheduled visits to the clinic.

[a] For background on financing and national health insurance see the chapters by John A. Butler and Theodore Marmor in volume III of this series.

The poor have another "time" problem because of the more institutionalized or bureaucratic settings in which they receive care. Alberta Parker cites

> long waiting times, difficulties in making appointments, impersonal treatment, little regard to cultural characteristics, frequent change in physicians and nurses, complex bureaucratically-oriented policies, demeaning eligibility procedures, and a maze of buildings and clinics to be navigated, fragmented services, no clearly identifiable entry procedures, and the inability to reach a provider when needed (Parker, 1974, p. 52).

These problems compound the difficulties facing poor families who seek primary care. The time the poor must travel to secure health care is simply greater than for the nonpoor. As measured by the 1969 Health Interview Survey, most visits to physicians by children from higher-income families required travel times of from one to fifteen minutes, whereas the poor were more likely to travel from fifteen to thirty minutes (though not often over thirty minutes) to reach their care providers.

The whole process of getting their children to a health care provider, from start to finish, is likely to require more planning, consume more time, and create more difficulties for poor than for well-to-do families. The comparison between a typical visit to a doctor in private practice and to a clinic illustrate this. It is highly likely that the child visiting the office of a physician will have had the appointment made on the same day, will go there in the family car, and will wait less than fifteen minutes to see the doctor. The child visiting the clinic, on the other hand, will have had the appointment made at least several days in advance, will not have used the family car to get there, and will wait more than fifteen minutes to see the doctor.

Utilization rates, alone, do not necessarily reveal the appropriateness of the medical services received by children. The primary medical care needs of children from well-to-do families are taken care of primarily by private physicians, whereas poor and nonwhite children rely more and more on clinics and other institutional settings. Lower-income and minority children rely on hospital, health care centers, and other institutional providers of medical services. Seventy-one percent of the white children who have a regular source of care receive care at physicians' offices; only 45 percent of nonwhites report similar regular sources of care (Table 5—3).

This does not necessarily imply that children from lower-income families receive a lower quality of care. The quality of diagnosis and treatment in institutional settings may well be equivalent to, or higher than, that supplied by private practitioners. But it does say a

Table 5–3. Sources of Regular Medical Care for Children by Age, Family Income, and Other Characteristics, 1972 *(Percent)*

	Source			
	Physician	*Clinic*	*Osteopath or Other*	*No Regular Source*
All	67	21	5	7
Age				
0–4	71	19	4	6
5–9	65	24	4	7
10–14	66	19	7	7
Family Income				
$0–5999	44	37	5	15
6000–10,999	69	17	6	8
11,000–45,000	75	18	5	2
Race				
White	71	18	6	5
Nonwhite	45	38	2	16
Residence				
SMSA—central city	56	31	4	9
SMSA—other	75	14	5	6
Urban—nonSMSA	71	24	2	3
Rural	70	17	7	6
Region				
Northeast	81	8	6	5
North Central	58	32	5	5
South	70	17	5	8
West	53	32	5	10

Source: "1970 Survey of Health Care Utilization and Expenditures," Center for Health Administration Studies of the University of Chicago in collaboration with the National Opinion Research Center. For a general discussion of survey findings among all age groups, see Andersen et al., *Health Service Use: National Trends and Variations*, DHEW Publication Number (HSM) 73–3004, October 1972.

good deal about the lack of regularity and continuity of care available to poor children who must use larger and more impersonal settings as their source of care. Furthermore, there is the question of the appropriateness of the care received in large institutions, which are more likely to stress technological diagnosis and the curing— rather than the caring—function of medicine.

Even more disturbing is the number of children who have no usual source of care. As shown in Table 5–3, approximately 7 percent (four million) of the children in the United States do not have a regular source of medical care. Children in low-income families are almost eight times as likely to have no regular source than those in affluent families; nonwhites more than three times as likely as whites, and those living in central cities one and one-half times as likely as those in suburbs.

Having a regular source of care is an important determinant of medical care utilization. Several studies have found that those with a regular source of care have rates of utilization of medical services more appropriate to their symptoms than those without a regular provider. Those who use a regular source, for example, are more likely to respond to symptoms according to the required level of medical care needed. A regular source of care also tends to encourage the use of preventive care. Another study indicates that having a regular source of care actually tends to stimulate increased utilization.

If the health care system is to provide appropriate levels and kinds of primary care, it must provide access to regular sources of care for both lower-income and higher-income children. These sources of care must be such that appropriate patterns of utilization are encouraged, and this requires that they must be available to lower-income children without cost.

Chapter 6

Getting Adequate Numbers
of Primary Care Practitioners

Despite evidence that primary care for children should emphasize the whole child and be able to recognize and deal with an increasing breadth of conditions, practitioners are becoming more specialized. Where primary care delivery sites should be brought as near to potential clients as possible, particularly to poor children, the trend is toward concentration of medical care delivery in larger institutions and therefore toward greater client-to-provider distances. Where chronic conditions and relatively mild acute illnesses comprise an even larger proportion of all childhood illnesses, the medical care system moves toward settings of higher technology aimed at treating less frequent conditions. Where a regular source of care is increasingly of central importance in organizing services effectively for individual children, the system moves toward greater impersonalization, fragmentation, and disjointedness. And where the need is to reach out and seek children who are in need of medical care and treatment, and to follow up on them once a treatment has been prescribed, the system tends to be passive and reactive.

These trends have not yet dominated the pattern of children's health care utilization. Children continue to rely primarily on private practitioners in office-based practice to supply their primary care needs (Table 6–1). Approximately two-thirds of all visits by children to health care providers for primary care are made to general practitioners, pediatricians, and internists in both solo and group practice.

Table 6—1.   Estimated Annual Visits to Private and Public Ambulatory Services, Early 1970s

Type of Service	Total Population		Children Under 15		
	Millions of Visits	Percent of Total	Millions of Visits	Percent of Total	Percent Omitting Schools and Public Health Clinics From Total
Private practice					
Solo	545	49.5	138.7	49.2	60.3
Group	185	16.8	44.5	15.8	19.3
	730	66.3	183.2	65.0	79.6
Hospital outpatient departments	200	18.2	32.9[a]	11.7	14.3
School and college health services	55	5.0	36.7	13.0	(omitted)
Industrial health units	40	3.6	----	----	----
Public health clinics	30	2.7	15.0	5.3	(omitted)
Special government programs	25	2.3	8.9	3.2	3.9
Special voluntary agencies	20	1.8	5.0	1.8	2.2
Total	1100	99.9[b]	281.7	100.0	100.0

[a] Includes emergency room visits.   [b] Total of percentages is 99.9 because of rounding.

Source: M. Roemer, "From Poor Beginnings, the Growth of Primary Care," *Hospitals* 49 (1 March 1975): 38. Extrapolations from these figures for children under fifteen by John A. Butler, "National Health Insurance and Primary Medical Care for Children" (unpublished doctoral dissertation, Graduate School of Education, Harvard University, Cambridge, Mass., 1976), pp. 25–27.

About 20,000 physicians (in terms of full-time equivalents) in office-based settings serve children.[a]

In terms of sheer volume of contacts with clients, public sector programs provide a larger share of children's services than of adult services. Public programs account for an estimated 23 percent of all ambulatory visits by children, compared to only about 15 percent by all age groups. In the public sector, neighborhood health centers provide comprehensive health care services, but their numbers of personnel in terms of full-time equivalents are still relatively small. The far more extensive public school and health department programs have a relatively limited function of providing screening, immunization, and other preventive care to millions of infants and children. These programs are only infrequently involved in handling acute illness or treating chronic conditions. Public school and health department programs employ 2500 physicians (in terms of full-time equivalents), and more than 25,000 nurses and nonphysician health practitioners.[b]

Because school and health department programs make contact with so many millions of children, they play an important role in providing health care—particularly preventive care—to American children. But these contacts or visits cannot be given equal weight in a qualitative sense with those visits paid by children to physicians and other practitioners in office-based and hospital-based practice. Visits to physicians in school or public health programs are almost invariably short in duration and for specific and limited purposes, often simply a brief physical examination.

A truer picture of the more comprehensive role of private practice in primary care services for children therefore emerges if visits to school and health department programs are removed from the percentages in Table 6—1. The private, office-based sector can then be seen to account for about 80 percent of the comprehensive services delivered to children. On the same basis, hospital out-patient departments account for only about 14 percent of these services.

As observed in Chapter 2, the forces at work in the primary care field are making significant changes in the numbers and kinds of physicians available for children's primary care, and they are having an impact on where these physicians are available. In turn, these changes

[a]The issue of the adequacy of present providers of primary health care is addressed in the chapter by Judy Baumann and David Calkins, M.D., in volume III of this series.

[b]The current structure of the health care delivery system for children is discussed more fully in the chapter by Elaine Baxter and John A. Butler in volume III of this series.

are having an important effect on the character and suitability of the medical services received by children. Briefly, there are not enough of the right kinds of doctors and other medical personnel in the right places to adequately respond to the primary health care needs of children.

IS THERE A PHYSICIAN "SHORTAGE"?

Many observers now concede that there is no over-all shortage of physicians in the United States. There has been a long historical growth trend in the ratio of physicians to the population (Figure 6-1). From 1931 through 1973, the numbers of active physicians increased from 159,000 to 351,000, the ratio of physicians per 100,000 population from 128 to 164. In the past few years, the increase in the ratio has accelerated to a pace beyond that experienced over the past half-century.

There have been two plateaus in the upward trend since 1931. The first occurred during and just after World War II. The second occurred in the mid-1950s and was attributable in large part to the pressures of the postwar population explosion on medical services as well as on schools and other institutions. The resumption of a steeper incline in the growth of the ratio of physicians to population since the late 1960s is due not only to a tapering off of the rate of population growth but also to public policies that resulted in increased immigration and training of physicians.

The relaxation of U.S. immigration laws in the mid-1960s was one such factor; this brought into the country an increasing number of foreign medical graduates from all parts of the world, especially from the Asiatic countries in recent years (Macy Commission, 1976). Foreign medical graduates as a percent of new physicians rose from 18 percent in 1963 to 45 percent in 1973. At present, nearly 25 percent of all active patient-care physicians in the United States and 40 percent of full-time hospital physician staffs are foreign medical graduates.

A second factor was the national decision to increase public funding of the training of physicians. This began with the Health Professions Educational Assistance Act of 1963, which authorized direct aid (capitation grants) to medical schools. Other legislation has also been enacted and funded to provide scholarship and loan as well as institutional and other kinds of assistance for the training of doctors and other health care professionals. These laws include the Health Manpower Act of 1968, the Comprehensive Health Manpower Train-

Figure 6–1.   Active Physicians per 100,000 Population, 1931 and 1973, Primary and Nonprimary Care Providers.

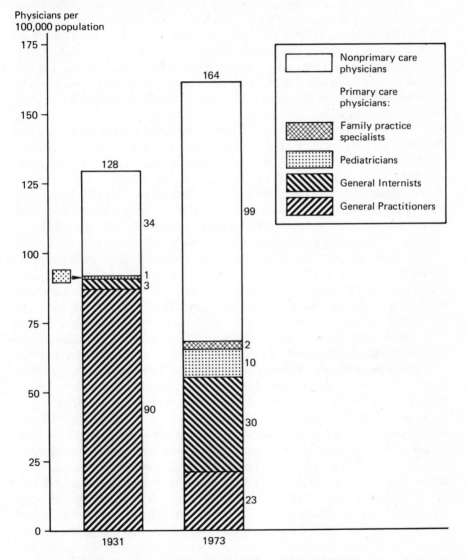

Source: Adapted from Macy Commission, 1976, and Roback, 1974.

ing Act of 1971, and the Health Professions Educational Assistance Act of 1976.

The cumulative effect of these measures has been to encourage far greater increases in the enrollment of students in medical schools than had been anticipated a few years ago. The number of first-year students rose from 11,300 to 15,300 between 1970 and 1975. Meanwhile, the increase in the numbers of residencies in hospitals increased by 82 percent—from 29,500 to 53,500—between 1964 and 1974. There is now a danger, says a report by the Carnegie Council on Policy Studies in Higher Education, that medical schools will become overbuilt in terms of the future demands for physicians in the United States (Carnegie Council, 1976).

But the upward surge in the over-all numbers of physicians has not resulted in similar increases in personnel delivering primary care or children's care in general. As can be seen in Figure 6—1, the ratio per 100,000 population of physicians providing primary care has declined, from 94 per 100,000 in 1931, to 65 per 100,000 in 1973. This decline has been mainly the result of the long historical decline in the number of general practitioners, from 112,000 in 1931 (72 percent of all active physicians) to 48,000 in 1973 (14 percent).

This over-all decline in primary care physicians understates the downward trend in the amount of children's primary care actually provided. In the first place, only GPs and family practitioners give most if not all their time to primary care. Thirty percent of pediatricians are in hospital-based practice and devote very little of their time to primary care; another 10 percent are in research, administrative, or other institutional settings. Further, for children the increase in internists, who see children infrequently, has not had much of an effect. Table 6—2 shows the numbers of full-time equivalent physicians loosely called primary care physicians who serve children.

In 1931 there were about 18.6 physicians (FTEs) per 100,000 who devoted time to primary care for children. This ratio had declined to 11.3 per 100,000 in 1973. There has been considerable expansion in recent years in the numbers of specialists who also provide primary care services. Pediatricians increased from 14,000 in 1963 to 21,000 in 1973, internists from 39,000 to 62,000, family practitioners from essentially zero to 6000. Altogether this group of primary care specialists in 1973 now accounted for 27 percent of all active physicians. However, increases in this group did not offset the steep decline in the numbers of GPs. In total, the group of physicians providing primary care services dropped from 49 to 42 percent of all active physicians, and the ratio of these physicians to the total population also declined (Macy Commission, 1976).

Nor are these specialists redressing the serious geographical maldistributions that affect primary care. The ratio of primary care physicians to population varies enormously by region and by density of population within regions. In 1970, the number of physicians per 100,000 population ranged from 74 GPs and other family doctors and 13 pediatricians in the East South Central region to 109 and 23 respectively in the Pacific states. Ratios ranged from 104 GPs and family doctors and 3 pediatricians in nonmetropolitan areas to 112 and 24 for the largest urban areas. And within these areas, many counties were without any medical practitioners, and poverty city areas had few or no doctors. There has been no significant improvement in this picture in the past five years. Nor is there likely to be if present patterns of behavior and training in the medical profession persist.

BEHAVIORAL PATTERNS
OF PEDIATRICIANS

The newer specialists who are coming to dominate the primary care field have very different professional styles than do general practitioners. Pediatricians are classified as specialists, and not unexpectedly they tend to behave more like specialists than GPs.

More pediatricians tend to gravitate towards institutional modes of practice, particularly towards hospitals. Those who do go into office-based practice favor group practice more than do GPs. Only one-fourth of private practice pediatricians were in some form of group practice in the early 1960s; today, the proportion is more than half, and a third of these are in multispecialty groups. As is also true of specialists in general, a relatively higher proportion of pediatricians go into research and other support activities in large medical institutions and complexes.

This tendency of pediatricians to behave as specialists has both favorable and unfavorable impacts on primary care for children. For example, in terms of efficiency and productivity in the delivery of care, group practice is generally a promising development. Practicing in groups and in institutions also keeps doctors in touch with new developments in medicine, and this probably improves their skills and abilities. On the other hand, the gravitation toward large institutions such as hospitals makes primary care less accessible to many people, more fragmented, and hence less suitable to children's needs. Pediatricians, like other specialists, charge higher fees than GPs and they tend not to establish practices in the central city. Private care for the central city poor is almost always GP care, care by another

Table 6–2.   Full Time Equivalent Child Health Physicians Serving Children, 1973

Type of Physician	Number[a]	Fraction of Time Spent Delivering Children's Primary Care	Number Full Time Equivalent Child Health Physicians
General Practitioner	48,192	.19[b]	9,156
Pediatrician	20,849	(.94)[b] (.58)[c]	11,367
General Internist	61,735	.03[b]	1,852
Family Practice	5,754	.19[d]	1,093
		Total	23,468

Sources: [a] Roback, 1974.
[b] National Center for Health Statistics, 1974 (percentage of time spent seeing children).
[c] Parker, 1974 (percentage of pediatricians in office-based, i.e., primary care).
[d] Estimated to be same as general practitioner, since family practice specialty not included in National Ambulatory Medical Care data.

type of specialist, or care by a non-board-certified physician. Or it occurs increasingly in an institutional setting.

This latter development has a major impact on the continuity of care for children. The staffing of a hospital outpatient department changes; different nurses, residents, interns, and specialists are available at the outpatient department at different times. Primary care for children in hospitals provided by the part-time efforts of hospital-based pediatricians along with the services of other specialists and personnel means that primary care in hospitals is most often the occasional activity of many, rather than the full-time activity of some.

An ambulatory patient "with a complex condition may receive the most up-to-date treatment in specialty clinics," observes Margaret Olendzki. But the orientation towards specialty services is apt to serve less well the general medical patient or the child in need of general pediatric care and well-child care. "The general medical clinic," she says, "tends to hold a particularly low status in the outpatient department and to accumulate patients with a number of commonly encountered health problems, many of a chronic nature" (Olendzki, 1975, pp. 27–28).

There is widespread recognition of the inadequacies of hospitals in handling ambulatory and primary care. A 1974 survey of some 4000 community hospitals indicated that the majority of these hospitals were actively working on or planning the development, expansion, or reorganization of ambulatory care services, but less than a quarter of them at present had outpatient departments; the large majority had only emergency rooms. Relatively few hospitals at present have the base on which to build adequate primary care services. This offers many hospitals the opportunity, in effect, of starting from scratch in building effective and productive primary ambulatory care services.

The lack of a well-established system of primary care may be helpful in facilitating moves toward a primary care system more responsive to children's needs. But it is evident that far-reaching solutions must be sought if the over-all downward trend in the supply of primary care physicians is to be remedied, if the primary-care services are to be more appropriate for the needs of children, and if they are to be delivered where children are. If these objectives are to be accomplished, different policy directions than those currently underway will have to be taken. New policies are needed to influence the training of medical professionals and the staffing of delivery units. The solutions that may work well for adult primary care—though none have worked very well up to now—may not produce the best results for children.

ARE MORE PHYSICIANS NEEDED?

In order to develop a manpower policy for getting the right amounts and kinds of personnel in the right places to take care of children's primary care needs adequately, the question has to be asked: What is the right number? The answer depends on what model of care is used.

The mode of care provided by many prepaid group practices is generally recognized as an effective and efficient model. If the ratio of physicians to population were the average of selected pre-paid groups (20 physicians per 100,000), the required number of physicians for children's primary care in 1980 would be 46,000. A higher estimate is arrived at by applying standards based on professional judgment of the services needed for good medical care. Using one set of such standards yields a ratio of 37 physicians per 100,000 population. That would indicate a need for 85,000 primary care children's physicians by 1980.

New physicians are now graduating from medical schools at the rate of about 11,500 a year and this number is increasing. About 1200 of these new graduates are entering pediatric residency programs and a slightly smaller number are becoming family physicians. Even with the trend toward more primary care providers, it is evident that without policy changes the number of physicians will not be sufficient to fulfill the needs for children's primary care personnel. New policy initiatives are being widely discussed and, in some cases, implemented. For example, federal legislation has established measures to induce students to enter the field of primary care. By 1980, half of the residencies at teaching hospitals must be in general or family practice and pediatrics—or the medical school will lose federal student grant funds. This requirement will shift more medical students into the primary care field.

Furthermore, all medical students must now enlist in the National Health Service Corps as a condition for receiving aid, or students must agree to serve two years of service in a particular location or forfeit a sum three times the amount of scholarship aid they receive, plus interest (*New York Times*, 13 October 1976). The effect of these service commitment requirements is uncertain. A survey of state scholarship and loan programs designed to attract students into rural communities found that 40 percent of all students who participated elected to buy out of the commitment or were in default of loan repayment. Further, of those who *did* repay their loan by working in rural areas, many probably would have chosen rural practice anyway, without any inducements (Mason, 1971).

In general, policies aimed at increasing primary care physicians by encouraging general increases in the physician population will be relatively ineffective and very costly. Policies that aim at increasing the share of medical school graduates going into primary care practices can be effective if they create strong incentives or restrictions for serving in areas of provider scarcity.

THE POSSIBILITY OF INCREASING NONPHYSICIAN HEALTH PRACTITIONERS

If the aim is to increase the primary care services available to children, a second strategy can also be applied, namely to expand the productivity of doctors and extend their activities through the use of nonphysician health practitioners. There is enormous opportunity for this kind of substitution among types of personnel. Primary care for children is not only highly labor-intensive, but also physician-intensive because of the way that office-based practice is generally carried out.

Pediatric nurse practitioners (PNPs) are one kind of personnel that can supplement physician services. They are registered nurses with sufficient additional training to enable them to provide well-child care, diagnose and treat common illnesses, counsel parents, and handle problems generally presented to primary care physicians over the phone. It is theoretically possible for one PNP, working under a pediatrician's supervision, to take on enough functions to increase the physician's productivity by as much as 75 percent. The actual increase in physician productivity resulting from use of PNPs has been found to be about 30 percent, a large increase in itself (Baker, 1970).

The training of PNPs is neither long nor costly, taking less than a year and costing about $4000. If the productivity of three PNPs is about equal to that of one pediatrician, the cost of producing the equivalent of one child health physician would be about $12,000. This compares favorably with the $75,000 estimated cost of a residency in family health care.

As of 1977, 3300 PNPs had been trained and about sixty programs were graduating some thousand new PNPs annually. On the basis of the favorable attitudes that pediatricians have expressed in surveys about PNPs, it has been estimated that by 1980 some 12,000 to 16,000 PNPs could be absorbed by pediatricians in private practice.

This would indicate that PNP training programs could be substantially expanded. But there are serious doubts about whether this number of physicians' assistants could or would be absorbed into the primary care system. Among the obstacles to the full utilization of PNPs in the delivery of care are inefficient personnel practices within the pediatric profession itself, and legal and statutory restrictions.

CHANGING PEDIATRICIANS' HABITS

In general pediatricians in private practice do not put their own time to the most effective use, nor do they delegate tasks extensively. According to one study, the median number of people employed by solo practitioners is two, while the median number for groups of two pediatricians is between three and four. These are not apt to be people who are highly skilled professionally. The most common types of employees are, first, secretaries, then "medical assistants" (most often trained on the job), and then registered nurses. In fact, only a little more than half of pediatricians (57 percent) employ RNs (Yankauer et al., 1970).

Physicians spend a large amount of time in nonpatient care activities and clinical activities requiring limited training and skill. They seldom delegate such patient-care tasks as information giving, information seeking, counseling, or assessment of physical condition, some of which could be done by nonphysicians. Similarly, registered nurses do not tend to spend more time with patients than do their lesser trained colleagues. Only 21 percent of the RN's workday is spent with patients, according to one study (Patterson and Bergman, 1969). The Subcommittee on Pediatric Manpower of the Council on Pediatric Practice of the American Academy of Pediatrics found that the inappropriate assignment of RNs to technical, clerical, and laboratory tasks capable of being handled by less highly trained personnel is an "extensive" problem.

Consequently, the introduction of PNPs or other nonphysician health practitioners into the current system of primary care will not result in substantial productivity gains if it occurs without major changes in the organization of care. As nonphysician health practitioners become increasingly available, physicians undoubtedly will welcome the chance to hire them because of their special skills. But the chances are that the PNP or other practitioner will simply tend to become a replacement for the present nurse, functioning much as the RN now does. And physicians' enthusiasm for PNPs may well wane when the period of innovation and experimentation is over and larger numbers of such personnel are in search of employment.

It is evident that if PNPs or other nonphysician health practitioners are to be utilized to their full potential, the groundwork for the major transformation of physicians' work habits must be laid in medical schools. Medical schools curricula should give greater stress to what might be summed up as the "management" of medical practices. This would emphasize the team aspects of medicine and the ways in which procedures can be delegated—in brief, the skills of supervision and management. Provision should be made to expose physicians-in-training to assistants. This might be considerably aided by the establishment of demonstration projects, perhaps in the form of clinics with nonphysician health practitioners on their staffs. This is in keeping with a recommendation made by the Carnegie study group regarding the need to reform curriculum so that students are given early clinical experience (Carnegie Council, 1976).

The implications of such an approach therefore are more far-reaching than that of merely an expansion of medical students. To utilize physicians' assistants effectively requires the restructuring of staffing patterns, the altering of physicians' traditional practices and habits. Something more is also required: financial incentives to promote the use of non-physician health practitioners, and legal and legislative changes to permit them to employ their skills effectively and fully.

LEGAL AND STATUTORY BARRIERS

Many states have restrictive licensure and certification requirements that deter the use of nonphysician health personnel. Many also have onerous regulations that prescribe the ways in which the assistants can and cannot perform tasks. Similarly, Medicaid regulations require that direct supervision must take place in the same office, thus limiting efficient use of the new professional personnel. In many cases, there are also regulatory restraints on the payment policies of third-party payers, such as Blue Cross. The net effect of these limitations is to restrict physicians' fees to services directly carried out under their supervision; services performed by nonphysician health professionals cannot be billed separately.

All these restrictive measures inhibit the use of PNPs and other assistants by physicians. Thus, the chance for increasing productivity in primary care will be lost if these restrictive measures are perpetuated.

Single billing cuts both ways, working against the best interests of both physician and consumer. In effect, the physician is faced with a choice of charging too little or too much for his services. If he covers the cost of the assistant's services in his own fee (as he does in the case of the services of his nurse), he decreases his income by hiring an assistant at a higher salary. However, to charge for the services of the assistant as though they were his own, as the Committee for Economic Development points out, "implies billing for an assistant's services at the going physician fee when the use of physicians' assistants might justify a lower rate than that charged for a physician's direct services" (1973, pp. 83–84). This would act to inflate medical costs still further. Separate billing for assistants' services therefore would appear to be a desirable objective of public policy aimed at removing obstacles to productive reshaping of organizational patterns of primary care.

As we have seen, the widespread use of assistants appears to be a worthwhile strategy for improving the effectiveness of primary care for children and for correcting the shortages of service providers. But specially trained assistants will be used only to the extent that the preferences of physicians, consumers, market-pricing mechanisms, and state regulations allow. High priority should be given to removing obstacles to the employment and use of nonphysician health personnel in all primary-care settings and to reshaping patterns of medical practice to accommodate their skills and talents. But these, it should be warned, are long-range objectives; institutional reforms cannot be accomplished in a few years.

Chapter 7

Getting Primary Care Services
Where They Are Needed

The limitations in the system that supplies primary health care to children are not represented solely by the aggregate numbers of providers. Not all people and places are affected equally by the aggregate shortages. Lower-income children in central cities do not receive adequate levels of primary care services, in part because their families cannot afford them. Another reason for their inadequate service utilizations is that primary care practitioners tend not to locate in the central cities. Rural communities also are affected by the tendency of practitioners not to locate in them. Increasing the affordability of primary care for lower-income families and the physical accessibility of service providers to central city and rural families should be two orientations of efforts to improve the responsiveness of the medical care system to children's needs.[a]

In 1975, total health care expenditures for children under nineteen were $15.4 billion, or $212 per capita. In comparison, total expenditures for all ages were $103.2 billion, or $476 per capita. Support for children's care is primarily provided by families—76 percent of all expenditures (Mueller and Gibson, 1976). Thus, it is not surprising that service providers tend to locate in higher-income, suburban communities.

---

[a]For background to this chapter, see the chapters coauthored by John A. Butler in volume III. Also see "Policy for Primary Medical Care for Children," by David S. Mundel, in volume III.

CURRENT EFFORTS TO INCREASE
AFFORDABILITY AND ACCESSIBILITY

Table 7—1 shows the breakdown of federal and state expenditures for personal health care. The intervention of the federal government in child health care has focused on both the affordability and accessibility of the "system" that delivers medical care to children. Federal expenditures on children are channeled through two main streams of funding to providers. One stream of funding that focuses primarily on affordability goes through the Medicaid program, which largely supports fee-for-service providers of care in the private sector. The other flows through a complex of categorical programs that support the delivery of medical services by providers in the public sector. In general, these services are provided to children and families without out-of-pocket charges. At different times, the federal government has used different kinds of categorical programs in an effort to close the gaps in the delivery of medical services to children. Many of the programs are not adequately or securely funded, and there is often no continuity or connection between them, not to mention linkups with programs in the private sector.

There are two major groups of categorical programs (not including the special comprehensive care programs for children of armed forces personnel and Indian children). One group is targeted mainly to providing or supporting specific kinds of medical services: dental services, aid to crippled children, and like programs. A large proportion of these services are provided by public health departments and schools. Most of these programs affecting children are funded under Title V of the Social Security Act. The second and newer group of programs generally support demonstration projects and offer more comprehensive medical services to disadvantaged families and children in urban areas. These programs have come into being since the mid–1960s.

There are no less than nineteen major federal programs that finance or provide health services for children and expectant mothers (Children's Defense Fund, 1976). These are funded not only by Title V of the Social Security Act but also under the authority of the Public Health Service, the Economic Opportunity Acts, and the Medicaid sections of the Social Security Act (Title XIX). They are administered by nine different federal agencies. In general, these programs involve joint federal-state supervision, regulation, and financial support. The requirement of state matching funds increases the amount of over-all public funds flowing into children's medical services by about a third. But it also adds a welter of complications to

Table 7—1. Estimated Personal Health Care Expenditures Under Public Programs, by Program and Source of Funds, for Children Under 19 and All Ages, 1975

Program	All Ages			Under 19		
	Total	Federal	State and Local	Total	Federal	State and Local
Total	$40,924	$28,578	$12,346	$3,749	$ 2,391	$1,358
Health insurance for the aged and disabled	14,121	$14,121	------	3	3	----
Temporary disability insurance	73	------	73	----	----	----
Workmen's compensation (medical benefits)	1,830	51	1,779	----	----	----
Public Assistance (vendor medical payments)	12,487	6,692	5,795	2,098	1,125	974
General hospital and medical care	5,492	1,090	4,492	518	320	198
Defense department hospital and medical care (including military dependents)	2,989	2,989	------	726	726	----
Maternal and child health services	535	272	263	365	186	179
School health*	----	----	----	----	----	----
Veteran's hospital and medical care	3,206	3,206	----	----	----	----
Medical vocational rehabilitation	190	157	33	38	31	7

Source: Mueller and Gibson, June 1976, p. 23.

*School health costs cannot be distinguished from education costs and hence are not represented in this table.

an already confused situation—particularly for the clients of the system. And it creates great disparities and gaps in the services received and in the qualifications for receiving them.

In a number of localities, the funding of medical delivery through this combination of consumer and supplier subsidies has improved (sometimes dramatically) the health of children. But over all, the effects of this funding mix on the utilization and delivery of care to children through the public systems of health care delivery have been extremely uneven. This unevenness results both from faults in the underlying conception of these programs and from the low levels of financial support often provided to these activities.

SCHOOL AND PUBLIC HEALTH PROGRAMS

Public health agencies and school departments deliver the bulk of the health services provided directly by government agencies.

School health programs encourage or provide a large volume of preventive care. About half of the states require some form of immunization as a prerequisite for school entry. Another quarter of the states delegate authority for establishing immunization requirements to local boards of education and health. Forty-two states require some kind of screening or examination of school children. Eleven of these states require only limited screening procedures, usually vision and hearing tests, but most require a more general physical examination at least once during a child's school year. But almost no states or local agencies require or provide for any kind of follow-up.

Primary care in the schools is provided for the most part by nurses and auxiliary personnel specializing in learning-related vision and hearing examination programs. In 1971, there were 16,000 full-time school nurses in the United States; including part-time nurses, total nurse equivalents were about 18,000. Thus, school nurses comprise a major proportion of medical professionals involved in delivering children's primary care. A large number of physician hours are also spent in school-based primary care, for the most part in supervisory activities. Increasing the involvement of this large contingent of primary care practitioners in the full cycle of primary care, from problem recognition through follow-up, remains a task confronting efforts to improve the medical care system's responsiveness to children's needs.

The responsibilities of public health departments are diverse. The typical department may have in it more than forty functions that include the inspection of food purveyors and barbershops, jurisdiction over air pollution control and occupational health, and supervision of water and sewer conditions. Over all, public health departments receive almost 60 percent of their funds from local sources and the other 40 percent about equally from state and federal sources. Because of the vast numbers of people covered by these systems, their resources are spread very thinly. One study, based on reports from 60 percent of public health departments, showed that in 1966 the per capita expenditure was less than two dollars.

Child health care accounts for a quarter of the time spent by health department personnel. Their major involvement is in programs for crippled children, child health, maternal health, and family planning programs. They have traditionally had a substantial commitment to immunization and well-child care activities. There has been a trend for immunization and maternal health programs to expand through addition of federal money; screening programs have also been expanding. Some public health departments have also taken an active part in the federal demonstration programs; public health departments operate about a sixth of the neighborhood health centers, about a third of the Children and Youth projects, and three-quarters of the Maternal and Infant Care projects.

Aside from this participation in federally funded comprehensive care demonstration programs, local health departments have not been widely employed in delivering the full cycle of primary care to children. The major problems with health departments from the standpoint of new initiatives in primary care are their resource constraints and rigidities in organizational structure and orientation.

FEDERAL DEMONSTRATION PROJECTS

The best known of the federal demonstration projects are the neighborhood health centers, which were started and funded originally by the Office of Economic Opportunity during the early days of the poverty program. (They are now administered by the Bureau of Comprehensive Health Service Projects of the Health Services Administration.) These centers are intended to take care of the health needs of people of all ages; about 37 percent (475,000) of the clientele are children. Three-quarters of the centers serve a client population of about 10,000 people, and the three largest centers have 30,000 or more clients. The centers offer a wide range of services and are staffed by physicians, nurses, and other professionals. About 70 percent of all visits by clients to the centers are for medical purposes; physicians are present at about two-thirds of these visits (Butler, 1975).

The second type of demonstration projects are Children and Youth projects. About sixty of these centers give comprehensive medical care to about a half million children. Some centers also dispense prescription drugs, counsel parents, and provide supplemental food for child participants; many offer extensive dental care. The centers are open five days a week for complete services, and about fifteen are open for emergency or partial care twenty-four hours. As with the NHCs, size of the centers varies widely, from 1000 children to 40,000; median client population size is 4500.

Like the other two programs, the Maternal and Infant Care program is aimed at lower-income families. A high percent of clients are minority children and women; over half are black, and between 15 and 20 percent are Spanish-speaking. This program was concerned with the idea of combatting infant mortality in high-risk areas by offering comprehensive medical, nutritional, and dental services to expectant and new mothers and their young children. There are fifty-six MIC projects, with a clientele of about 141,000 women.

All three programs have given continuous and comprehensive care to deprived people in urban areas. Over-all utilization in the areas served by the program-supported sites has increased, and there are no wide-scale evidences of overutilization. Staffing of the centers on the whole appears to be satisfactory. The quality of care appears to be generally high. Many C and Y centers have been able to uncover and treat a large number of correctible defects in the children in their areas.

The attention attracted by these projects, particularly by the neighborhood health centers, is somewhat misleading in comparison with their over-all effects. Neighborhood health centers actually serve only about 3 percent of the urban poor who are regarded as their "target" population. The Maternal and Infant Care program serves 7 percent of its eligible population, and the Children and Youth projects, 4 percent.

Categorical funding by recurrent legislative acts is an inherently insecure form of funding for institutionally based programs. This insecurity has been a major problem frustrating development and expansion of the comprehensive delivery programs from the start. It was originally intended that both the neighborhood centers and the Children and Youth projects were to be financed through Medicaid, as are other providers of care to low-income people. But this was never fully implemented, with the result that today only about 15 percent of the financing of these two programs comes from Medicaid funds. If new delivery units are to be started and maintained as service providers in underserved areas, stable sources of financial support must be developed. This stability could be achieved either through increased fee-for-service reimbursement or more stable grant funding mechanisms.

THE EPSDT PROGRAM

The Early and Periodic Screening, Diagnosis and Treatment program for children was authorized after it became apparent that Medicaid was not well adapted to provide the full cycle of primary care that children particularly require. The Medicaid program was specifically amended to provide reimbursement for screening, diagnostic services, and treatment of children qualifying for Medicaid benefits. The purposes were admirable; the results have been disappointing.

Major problems were encountered at the outset. States did not wish to incur additional Medicaid cost-sharing responsibilities, and physicians did not wish to participate in the program because of low reimbursement schedules. There were lawsuits over compliance by the states, and Congress tried to remedy matters by tightening up the regulations. But as of now, less than half of the child population eligible for Medicaid has been reached—and that is only a portion of the total poverty population.

Because of the emphasis of EPSDT on prevention, the program lies in an area that has traditionally occupied the attention of the public sector. School systems in several states have set up screening, diagnostic, and treatment programs under these funds. But in most cases, they have not been able to qualify for reimbursement. There are various barriers. One is the difficulty of determining reimbursement formulas for school populations with some children eligible under welfare regulations and others not. Another is the Medicaid billing requirement in many states whereby only a physician may be reimbursed for services: this rules out reimbursement for nurses and other nonphysician practitioners who provide most in-school services.

Forced to implement the program by Congress, some state authorities have sought to comply by setting up a separate delivery apparatus for the program, duplicating services already provided. To set up separate programs for screening and delivery risks failure at the stage of referral, subsequent diagnosis, and treatment because of the lack of integration with the ongoing regular sources of care for the child. Thus, the EPSDT program that was set up to respond to the failure of Medicaid reimbursement to encourage the development of a full cycle of primary care has itself sometimes encouraged further fragmentation of the primary care system.

POLICY IMPLICATIONS

The nation has now had a decade of experience with various kinds of programs aimed at increasing people's ability to pay for medical services; improving their access to these services; and developing more trained medical personnel, and raising their productivity. These programs, both in the private and public sectors, have generally produced positive, although widely varying results. Often the results have been small in comparison with the problems at which they are aimed. In part, this can be attributed to the amount of funding that the nation has been willing to put behind a particular program; some programs simply have been given such low funding that nothing much could have been accomplished, regardless of the possibilities. In large part, however, it is also due to the kinds of incentives that have been employed in bringing providers and providing institutions into the programs.

Broadly, Medicaid has increased the utilization of health care services by poor children. But not all children of low-income and moderate-income families are covered, nor are they covered for all services, the main omission being services for primary—ambulatory and (especially) preventive—care. The fee-for-service reimbursement strategy of Medicaid tends to create incentives for fragmented services and to promote more institutionalized settings, whereas more continuity of service and informal and decentralized settings appear preferable for children's primary care. In like manner, the Medicaid fee-for-service structure tends to promote the use of more procedures (technological in nature) than are required in children's primary care at the same time that it discourages the use of follow-up services that are highly desirable for children. The constraints on the reimbursement of nonphysician health practitioners, such as pediatric nurse practitioners, inhibit the role these professionals could play in increasing the availability and productivity of the full cycle of children's care. In the main, the Medicaid fee-for-service reimbursements have not induced desired innovative changes in the mode or location of delivery of primary care.

Categorical assistance has been effective in creating and maintaining some innovative new delivery units that make extensive use of nonphysician health practitioners and are dispersed geographically nearer to clients in localities that need primary care services. But these tend to be large centers serving a big clientele, more institutional in character than necessary. The mode of funding tends to promote this because larger institutions with greater managerial resources have the capacity to handle the contract or grant funding process in the first place. If neighborhood programs were to be expanded through the use of categorical funding, the programs would have to be watched carefully in order to avoid an excessive institutional trend.

✳ *Chapter 8*

The Desirability of a Mixed
System of Financing

A number of proposals for widespread changes in the system of health care financing are currently under national consideration. Universal medical insurance coverage and wider benefits for all Americans through the intervention of the federal government have been proposed. Expansion of support for categorical mechanisms to support new forms of delivery have also been proposed. A number of bills embodying various approaches toward improved medical care are pending in Congress. In any attempt to analyze these proposals it must be borne in mind that children's concerns are not always the central issues around which these plans have been developed. Medical care for children differs from that for adults in its stress on the longitudinal aspects of primary care services. Programs and policies designed to fulfill children's needs do not adequately deal with all the consequences and problems of the increasingly expensive, hospital-based, sophisticated services that most Americans identify with modern medical care. Programs and policies designed to deal with the medical care needs of adults do not adequately respond to children's needs for primary care. A delicate balancing of interests is required.

If children's best interests are to be fostered, health care financing proposals should be examined carefully in light of children's special needs. Very broadly, if it is to be responsive to children's needs, reform of the medical financing and delivery system should work toward: (1) increased utilization of primary care services by children from low-income and moderate-income families, particularly those in now underserved urban and rural areas; (2) expanded delivery of care in settings close to clients; (3) greater use of pediatric nurse practitioners and other nonphysician health care professionals who can contribute productively to many functions of primary care; (4) increased provision of a regular source of care for each child; and (5) wider emphasis in the cycle of care from a narrow focus on diagnostic procedures and therapy to problem recognition and follow-up. To avoid high program costs, controls that limit total costs are also desirable.

If it can be assumed that these objectives are important, the task is then to examine medical care financing proposals in terms of the incentives they create—or do not create—among providers and consumers of primary health care for the desired outcomes. Four questions can be asked: Are the incentives appropriate? (Do they correspond in direction and purpose with the outcomes that are sought?) Are they effective? (Do they cause the desired outcomes in children's primary care to occur?) Are they efficient? (Do they cause more of the desired outcomes to occur than an alternative approach that might have been taken instead?) Finally, are they adequate? (Is the level of the outcomes stimulated that which is desired?)

The proposals for reform of the financing of health care that are now being actively considered vary widely in the services included for which they would provide reimbursement; the ways they would restructure reimbursement to providers; the incentives they would create; and the effects these would have on children's primary care. The benefits allowed by these plans vary widely in the share of medical costs covered and the range of services permitted within the allowed coverage. The beneficiaries to be covered are another important variable. So is the mode of reimbursement, whether it would be fee-for-service, capitation payments to providers who enroll individuals for comprehensive sets of services, or a mixture of the two. All these differences have important effects on children. Other attributes of the alternative plans, such as who would administer the program (federal government, employers, private carriers) and how the program would be financed (general tax, payroll tax, employer contribution) would have somewhat less of an effect on children's care.[a]

[a]Material in this chapter is taken primarily from Theodore Marmor's chapter in volume III of this series.

NATIONAL HEALTH CARE FINANCING PROPOSALS

There are four basic types of national health care proposals. The first type would involve public or private insurance against major medical expenses, so-called catastrophic health insurance. This insurance could either be publicly or privately administered and financed, perhaps through the expanded use of tax credits or deductions. This type of alternative would minimize direct government involvement in the medical care system.

Within this class of proposals are those providing federally subsidized insurance protection against financially catastrophic expenses. For example, hospitalization beyond sixty days and annual medical expenditures of more than $2000 would be covered.[a] A variant plan would provide comprehensive universal health insurance coverage with a very high deductible; it would pay all medical bills that exceeded 10 percent of annual income. The use in one form or another of a deductible high in relation to average yearly medical expenditures is intended to combat medical inflation with consumer restraint.

At the other extreme is a second type of plan which involves the creation of a government monopoly of the health insurance business and provides for universal eligibility and broad coverage of services financed by government subsidies.[b] There would be no cost-sharing by patients; care under the plan would be free at the point of service, with the federal government paying providers directly. Cost escalation could be controlled by limiting the total budget for medical care. Services could be redistributed by creating incentives for comprehensive health service organizations, e.g., health maintenance organizations, and for placing health personnel in underserved areas. Quality of services could be maintained by government regulation of the standards of care. This type of plan would involve intensive, far-reaching involvement by government agencies in the medical care system.

A third group of proposals involves a mixed strategy of increased government regulation and partial federal support for the medical care system. Such plans would mandate coverage for all people under some form of either a public or private insurance plan. Financial contributions of families would rise as the family incomes rise; costs would be controlled by state regulations; and prepaid group practice

[a]as in the Long-Ribicoff Bill before the 94th Congress.

[b]The prototype of this type of proposal is the Kennedy-Corman Bill before the 94th Congress.

would be encouraged. Employers would be required to offer policies with broad benefits; employees would pay some share of the premium and would be responsible for some cost-sharing at the time of use. Whatever their specific features, such plans share health expenditures among patients, employers, and government.

The inadequacies of the various plans developed under these three general categories have inspired further efforts to devise a fourth type of program that would give recognition to the special needs of children and of the poor. One approach that has been suggested, for example, would be to federalize Medicaid, getting rid of some of the objectionable features of the program that now result from the complex joint federal-state relationship, and simultaneously to strengthen the provision of primary care for children by increased funding of categorical programs that support new primary care units in underserved areas. Still another approach would be to bring about national health insurance in phases, starting with benefits for children; the first stage of this approach might involve comprehensive benefits for children and catastrophic insurance for other age groups.

BENEFICIARIES AND BENEFITS

Universal coverage under a national health program means that children will have to compete with other citizens whose effective demands for health care would also have been increased. To what extent will children's interests be hurt in this competition? Studies based on the Canadian experience with national health insurance indicate that, while the results are somewhat mixed, the negative consequences of such competition feared by some child advocates will not be borne out. Canadian data suggest that two developments in children's access to care are likely to occur under conditions of universal financial accessibility to health care. One is that poor children will improve their access somewhat relative to other children and that children as a class will consume more resources than before. The other likely result, however, may be that children compared to the elderly will use a slightly smaller proportion of total resources.

As discussed earlier in this report, the costs of primary care services for children are lower than the costs of care for other age groups; therefore, they are not apt to be covered by health insurance plans that have deductibles wherein the family pays for care up to a certain level of costs. Deductibles in an insurance plan, therefore, will not significantly reduce out-of-pocket costs for children. Therefore the pattern of care for most children would be unaffected by the enactment of a catastrophic or deductible insurance plan. Children as a whole may be negatively influenced by a catastrophic or high deductible insurance plan if it created further incentives for medical personnel to move away from primary care. It should be noted that catastrophic insurance could have a very significant effect in one area, namely, in its impact on the new medical technology and the treatment of severe illnesses that affect a small number of children. Hemophilia treatment and bone marrow transplants are illustrations of such highly specialized and expensive procedures. The catastrophic coverage approach, for example, provides an alternative source of funds beyond the current categorical and research support for tertiary care affecting small numbers of children. In this sense, such plans could make a valuable contribution to children's health care.

Any national health care program that does not specifically make provision for primary care services will have the indirect effect of reallocating resources toward areas other than primary care. Moreover, failure to reimburse for services provided by nonphysician professionals will further jeopardize the adequacy of the supply of primary care.

MODES OF REIMBURSEMENT
AND FINANCIAL INCENTIVES

If changes are to be made in the delivery system, a national health care financing program must be coupled with an active effort to start and nurture new delivery modes. It must embody provisions that will allow reimbursement of nontraditional personnel and institutions. It should have "allowable" fee schedules that will create incentives for cost reductions.

It should be added that none of the present proposals seems to offer sufficiently strong financial incentives to lure physicians and other medical care providers into areas of provider scarcity. Unless reimbursement formulas are heavily weighted to favor children in such areas, they are unlikely to have any impact on the distribution of, and hence access to, providers.

It is widely suggested that prepayment, especially as exemplified in the current financing system for health maintenance organizations and medical care foundations, is a good financing mode for children's care. Because care for children is predictable, outpatient-oriented, and low-cost, it seems ideal for prepayment through capitation. Incentives on providers to control costs and put limits on inappropriate hospital use are more effective, while consumer incentives to full use of available services are also stronger because no out-of-pocket costs result from visits. Consequently, adequacy of children's primary care may tend to be better assured in prepaid practice arrangements than other arrangements.

It should not be assumed, however, that prepaid practice arrangements will be as satisfactory and attractive to consumers under an expanded system of low- or no-deductible health insurance as they are at present. The advent of large-scale government involvement in payment for care complicates the relation of consumer to provider by adding a government agency as third party to underwrite some portion of care, especially for the poor and near poor, and to monitor the quality of care. The clearest precedent for this type of government involvement is the prepayment experience under Medicaid, which suggests that prepaid practice arrangements may have some special problems under a national health care financing scheme. First, insurance removes one of the incentives—control of out-of-pocket costs—for family interest in prepayment health arrangements. A comprehensive care scheme would be affected by the amount of patient turnover and the number of supplemental or redundant sources of care for which the patient would bear no cost. "Leakage" to other provider arrangements may undermine the cost control economies and care continuities of prepaid group practices. The government could attempt to avoid this problem by stipulating that consumers must use a single source of care. It seems unrealistic, however, to assume that any national health insurance bill could be passed forbidding supplementation or enforcing such a choice-restricting provision if it were included.

A mixed mode of reimbursement would appear to be the practical approach to the financing of children's primary health care services. While fee-for-service creates few incentives for delivery system changes, without fee-for-service payments many current providers would not participate in the system. Capitation would help create incentives, for delivery system change especially for new delivery modes in underserved areas. It encourages regularity of use by children, particularly of such services as follow-up, which are difficult to charge for in a fee-for-service system. A system that includes both fee-for-service and capitation payments seems required.

Presently, a large proportion of poor and near poor children receive preventive services in a local school, a health department clinic, or a federally-initiated program. Without the supplementary provision of services in schools, health departments, neighborhood health centers, and similar programs, these lower-income children would end up especially underserved. The question is how to provide support for these services in a mixed mode system of government payments.

Financing these programs by categorical funds, as noted in the previous chapter, is an insecure means of financing. Yet as also observed, neighborhood health centers, C and Y projects, and other new delivery institutions have not been generously supported by Medicaid, although this promises to be much easier under any plan which is fully federal. Should services now provided under federal matching programs be reimbursed solely or in part by third-party fee-for-service and capitation payments?

In some cases the answer could be that direct funding of public settings would be better than relying on the indirect mechanism of third-party payments. This would be particularly true where fee-for-service or capitation reimbursement fail to bring providers into an underserved area. This invites the duplication of services and inefficiency, but may be the best available means of ensuring medical service for children in some circumstances. A flexible reimbursement policy would make possible the use of different combinations of reimbursement according to different local or regional conditions. Presumably, public providers would be eligible for receiving third-party payments to finance the operating costs of primary care services.

EFFECT ON RESEARCH INTO THE
CYCLE OF CARE

Other important new directions should be sought in the areas of research and development. Clinical as well as systems research should emphasize as much as possible the effectiveness of primary care services and delivery modes and also the development of data to measure performance at all stages in the cycle of care. Although research is not commonly considered a part of the financing and delivery of medical services, policymakers should incorporate the funding and encouragement of research where possible into broad health care proposals. To the extent this occurs, the needs of children's primary care should be kept high on the agenda of basic and applied biomedical research.

References

Aday, L.A. "Economic and non-economic barriers to the use of needed medical services," *Med Care* 3 (1975): 447.

Aday, L.A. *The Utilization of Health Services: Indices and Correlates, A Research Bibliography, 1972.* DHEW Pub. No. (HSM) 73−3003. Washington, D.C.: National Center for Health Services Research and Development, 1972.

Aday, L.A. *Dimensions of Family's Social Status and Their Relationships To Children's Utilization of Health Services.* Johns Hopkins University Department of Medical Care and Hospitals, xerox, 1971.

Alpert, J.J., et al. "Effective use of pediatric care: Utilization of health resources," *Am J Dis Child* 116 (1968): 529.

Baker, A.J. "Editorial: Primary care by the nurse," *N Engl J Med* 283 (1970): 129.

Baumann, J., and Calkins, D. "Providing primary care practitioners for children," in *Developing a Better Health Care System for Children.* Cambridge, MA.: Ballinger Publishing Co., 1977.

Beauchesne, D., and Mundel, D.S. Determinants of utilization of children's health services," in *Developing a Better Health Care System for Children.* Cambridge, MA.: Ballinger Publishing Co., 1977.

Bennett, R. "Allocation of child medical care decisionmaking authority," in *Developing a Better Health Care System for Children.* Cambridge, MA.: Ballinger Publishing Co., 1977.

Bernick, K. "Issues in pediatric screening," in *Children's Medical Care Needs and Treatments.* Cambridge, MA.: Ballinger Publishing Co., 1977.

Butler, J.A. *Improving the Organization of Primary Medical Care Services for American Children.* Cambridge, MA.: Harvard Child Health Project, xerox, 1975.

Butler, J.A. "Financing children's health care," in *Developing a Better Health Care System for Children.* Cambridge, MA.: Ballinger Publishing Co., 1977.

Butler, J.A., and Baxter, E. "Current structure of the health care delivery system for children," in *Developing a Better Health Care System for Children.* Cambridge, MA.: Ballinger Publishing Co., 1977.

Carnegie Council on Policy Studies in Higher Education. *Progress and Problems in Medical and Dental Education: Federal Support versus Federal Control.* A report of the Carnegie Council on Policy Studies in Higher Education. New York: Jossey-Bass, 1976.

Children's Defense Fund. *Doctors and Dollars are not Enough: How to Improve Health Services for Children and Their Families.* Cambridge, MA.: Children's Defense Fund, 1976.

Committee for Economic Development. *Building a National Health System.* Statement on national policy by the Committee for Economic Development, New York, April, 1973.

Davis, K. "Medicaid payments and utilization of medical services by the poor," *Inquiry* 13 (1976): 127.

Dodge, W.F., et al. "Patterns of maternal desires for child health care," *Am J Public Health* 60 (1970): 1421.

Graef, J. "Lead Poisoning," in *Children's Medical Care Needs and Treatments.* Cambridge, MA.: Ballinger Publishing Co., 1977.

Graef, J. "Appendicitis," in *Children's Medical Care Needs and Treatments.* Cambridge, MA.: Ballinger Publishing Co., 1977.

Graef, J. "Streptococcal pharyngitis and rheumatic fever," in *Children's Medical Care Needs and Treatments.* Cambridge, MA.: Ballinger Publishing Co., 1977.

Haggerty, R.J., et al. *Child Health and the Community.* New York: John Wiley and Sons, 1975.

Kessner, D.M., et al. *Assessment of Medical Care for Children.* Contrasts in Health Status, vol. 3. Washington, D.C.: National Academy of Sciences, 1974.

Kimm, S.Y.S. "The case of tonsillectomy and adenoidectomy," in *Children's Medical Care Needs and Treatments.* Cambridge, MA.: Ballinger Publishing Co., 1977.

Longfellow, C., and Freeman, E. "Reading disability," in *Children's Medical Care Needs and Treatments.* Cambridge, MA.: Ballinger Publishing Co., 1977.

Macy Commission. *Physicians for the Future.* Report of the Macy Commission. New York: Josiah Macy Jr. Foundation, 1976.

Mason, H.R. "Effectiveness of student aid programs ties to a service commitment," *J Med Educ* 44 (1971): 575.

Marmor, T.R. "The politics of national health insurance proposals: what's in it for kids?" in *Developing a Better Health Care System for Children.* Cambridge, MA.: Ballinger Publishing Co., 1977.

Morris, N., et al. "Alienation as a deterrent to well-child supervision," *Am J Public Health* 5 (1966a): 1874–82.

Morris, N., et al. "Deterrents to well-child supervision," *Am J Public Health* 56 (1966b): 1232–41.

Mueller, M.S., and Gibson, R.M. "Age differences in health care spending, fiscal year 1975," *Social Security Bulletin* (June 1976): 18.

Mundel, D. "Policy for primary medical care for children," in *Developing a*

Better Health Care System for Children. Cambridge, MA.: Ballinger Publishing Co., 1977.

Newberger, E.H., et al. *Child Health In America: Toward a Rational Public Policy*. Advisory Committee on Child Development, 1976.

Olendzki, M.C. "What hospitals can do about primary care," in *Community Hospitals and the Challenge of Primary Care*. A report by the Center for Community Health Systems. New York: Columbia University Center for Community Health Systems, 1975.

Parker, A. "The dimensions of primary care: blueprints for change," in *Primary Care: Where Medicire Fails*, edited by S. Andreopoulis. New York: John Wiley and Sons, 1974.

Patterson, P.K., and Bergman, A.B. "Time-motion study of six pediatric office assistants," *N Engl J Med* 281 (1969): 771.

Roback, G.A. *Distribution of Physicians in the United States*, 1973. Chicago: American Medical Association, Center for Health Services Research and Development, 1974.

Roemer, M., et al. "Copayments for ambulatory care: pennywise and pound foolish," *Med Care* 13 (1975): 6.

Senior, B., and Smith, B.A. "The number of physicians as a constraint on the delivery of health care: how many physicians are enough?" *JAMA* 222 (1972): 178.

Starfield, B. "Efficacy and effectiveness of primary medical care for children," in *Children's Medical Care Needs and Treatments*. Cambridge, MA.: Ballinger publishing Co., 1977.

Starfield, B. "Iron deficiency anemia," in *Children's Primary Medical Care Needs and Treatments*. Cambridge, MA.: Ballinger Publishing Co., 1977.

Starfield, B. "Middle ear infection," in *Children's Primary Medical Care Needs and Treatments*. Cambridge, MA.: Ballinger Publishing Co., 1977.

Starfield, B. "Health needs of children," in *Children's Primary Medical Care Needs and Treatments*. Cambridge, MA.: Ballinger Publishing Co., 1977.

Talbot, N.B., and Guthrie, A. "Health care needs of American children," in *Raising Children in Modern America*, edited by N.B. Talbot. Boston, MA.: Little, Brown and Co., 1976.

Taylor, D.G., et al. "A social indicator of access to medical care," *J Health and Social Behavior* 16 (1975): 38.

Tompkins, R.F. "Children's advocacy in the health sector," in *Developing a Better Health Care System for Children*. Cambridge, MA.: Ballinger Publishing Co., 1977.

Tompkins, R.W., et al. *The Cost Effectiveness of Pharyngitis Management and Acute Rheumatic Fever*. Undated mimeograph, 1976.

Weiss, J.E., and Greenlick, M.R. "Determinants of medical care utilization: the effect of social class and distance on contacts with the medical care system," *Med Care* 8 (1970): 456.

Wennberg, J., and Kimm, S.Y.S. "Common uses of hospitals: A look at Vermont," in *Children's Medical Care Needs and Treatments*. Cambridge, MA.: Ballinger Publishing Co., 1977.

Yankauer, A., et al. "The practice of nursing in pediatric offices—challenge and opportunity," *N Engl J Med* 282 (1970): 843.